Gooseberry Patch co.

A Country Store In Your Mailbox®

Made from Scratch

A Country Store In Your Mailbox®

Gooseberry Patch
600 London Road
Department Book
Delaware, OH 43015

★

1-800-854-6673
gooseberrypatch.com

Copyright 2001, Gooseberry Patch 1-888052-87-2
First Printing, November, 2001

How To Subscribe

Would you like to receive
"A Country Store in Your Mailbox"®?
For a 2-year subscription to our 96-page
Gooseberry Patch catalog, simply send $3.00 to:

Gooseberry Patch
600 London Road
Delaware, OH 43015

Contents

Dedication

This book is dedicated to those who love the simple, homestyle dishes we grew up with.

Appreciation

A sincere "thanks" to all the terrific cooks who shared their best recipes with us!

Vanilla

Quilting Bee

Cranberry Scones

Sandy Halteman
Osceola, MO

Warm from the oven, these are heavenly split
and topped with butter.

1 c. sugar, divided
2-1/2 c. all-purpose flour
2-1/2 t. baking powder
1/2 t. baking soda

3/4 c. chilled butter, sliced
1 c. cranberries
1 c. buttermilk, divided

Combine 2/3 cup sugar, flour, baking powder and baking soda in a large mixing bowl; cut in butter until mixture resembles coarse crumbs. Fold in cranberries; stir in 3/4 cup buttermilk until just moistened. Turn dough onto a lightly floured surface and knead 6 to 8 times; divide dough in half. Pat each half into an 8-inch circle; cut each circle into 8 wedges. Brush tops with remaining buttermilk; sprinkle with remaining sugar. Transfer to an ungreased baking sheet; bake at 350 degrees for 15 minutes or until golden. Makes 16 servings.

Almond Tea

Diane Goering
Topeka, KS

So easy to make, enjoy it anytime.

1 c. sugar
2/3 c. lemon juice
1 t. almond extract

1 t. vanilla extract
1 T. instant tea
9 c. water

Combine all ingredients in a tea kettle; bring to a boil. Remove from heat and serve. Makes about 10 servings.

Pink Lady Pie

Virginia Sieberhogen
Shannon, IL

Sweet and tart...the perfect pie combination!

2 c. rhubarb, diced
1 c. sugar
3-oz. pkg. strawberry gelatin
1 T. lemon juice

2 c. whipped topping
9-inch graham cracker pie crust,
   unbaked

Combine rhubarb and sugar in a saucepan; cook on low heat until rhubarb is tender. Add gelatin and stir until dissolved; remove from heat and let cool. Stir in lemon juice; fold in whipped topping. Pour into prepared crust; chill until ready to serve. Serves 8.

Vintage salt shakers make great little containers to dust powdered sugar on baked goodies!

Triple Cheese Ball

Peggy Kuykendall
Crossville, IL

*Sometimes I shape the mixture into bite-size cheese
balls...just right for individual appetizers.*

2 8-oz. pkgs. cream cheese,
   softened
8-oz. pkg. sharp Cheddar
   cheese, grated
8-oz. pkg. crumbled blue cheese
1/2 onion, diced

1-1/2 T. Worcestershire sauce
2 T. crushed red pepper flakes
1-1/2 c. finely chopped pecans,
   divided
1-1/2 c. fresh parsley, chopped
   and divided

Blend together cheeses, onion, Worcestershire sauce and red pepper;
mix in one cup pecans and 1/2 cup parsley. Cover and chill one hour.
Shape into 4 balls. Combine the remaining pecans and parsley; roll
balls in the pecan mixture. Cover and chill until ready to serve. Makes
32 servings.

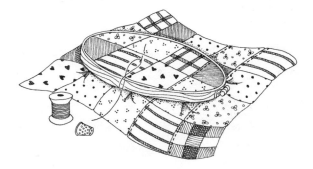

*Search flea markets and tag sales for vintage canning
jars...they're the right size to hold tiny spools of thread,
thimbles, needles and buttons.*

Creamy Blue Cheese Dip

Teresa Sullivan
Westerville, OH

*The blue cheese makes this a tasty dip for fresh veggies
or spread on warm slices of toasted French bread.*

3/4 c. sour cream
1/2 t. dry mustard
1/2 t. pepper
1/8 t. salt

1/3 t. garlic powder
1 t. Worcestershire sauce
1-1/3 c. mayonnaise
4-oz. pkg. crumbled blue cheese

In a medium mixing bowl, combine sour cream, mustard, pepper, salt, garlic powder and Worcestershire sauce; blend on low speed for 2 minutes. Add mayonnaise and blend on low for 30 seconds; increase to medium speed and blend an additional 2 minutes. Slowly add blue cheese; blend on low speed for no longer than 4 more minutes. Refrigerate for 24 hours before serving. Makes 2-1/2 cups.

*Teapot is on, the cups are waiting, favorite chairs are
anticipating. No matter what I have to do,
my friend, there's always time for you.*
-Unknown

Poppy Seed Cake

Beverly Neighorn
Grand Blanc, MI

An old-fashioned favorite...enjoy with a cup of chamomile tea.

2/3 c. shortening
1-3/4 c. sugar
2 eggs
1-1/2 t. vanilla extract
2-3/4 c. all-purpose flour

2-1/2 t. baking powder
1 t. salt
1-1/4 c. milk
1/3 c. poppy seed
Garnish: powdered sugar

Cream shortening, sugar, eggs and vanilla together in a large mixing bowl; beat 5 minutes. Combine flour, baking powder and salt in another mixing bowl; add alternately with milk to the sugar mixture. Stir in poppy seed; pour into a greased and floured 12-cup Bundt® pan and bake at 350 degrees for 50 to 55 minutes. Cool in pan 10 minutes; invert and cool on serving plate. Sprinkle with powdered sugar. Makes 12 servings.

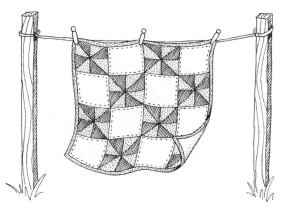

Turn mismatched cups upside down and place a pretty saucer on top to give each guest their own individual cake stand...a fun way to serve mini cheesecakes or cookies.

Lemon Butter

Kevin Scharff
Wilmington, DE

This adds an extra special touch when spread on warm scones, sweet rolls or quick breads.

5 eggs, beaten
2 c. sugar
juice and zest of 3 lemons

1/2 c. unsalted chilled butter, sliced

Place beaten eggs in top of double boiler; add sugar, lemon juice and zest. Cook until almost boiling; add butter slices, stirring constantly until melted and mixture coats back of spoon. Pour into 2, one-pint jars; allow to cool. Add lids and tighten; refrigerate and use within 2 weeks. Makes 2 pints.

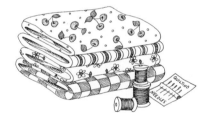

Sweet Brie Bake

Kathy Grashoff
Fort Wayne, IN

Especially good with pear or apple slices.

1/2 lb. Brie cheese
1/4 c. apricot jam

1/4 c. whole pecans

Remove rind from Brie and discard; place Brie in a small baking dish with rim. Pour jam over cheese; sprinkle with pecans. Bake at 350 degrees for 7 to 10 minutes or until warm and bubbling. Serves 4.

Cheesy Stuffed Mushrooms

Erin O'Shea
Morrison, CO

Try Italian or garlic bread crumbs for a different flavor.

1 lb. mushrooms
3 T. olive oil
2 T. onion, grated
1/2 t. dried tarragon
1/2 t. pepper

1/2 c. bread crumbs
1/2 c. shredded Swiss cheese
2 T. milk
2 T. grated Parmesan cheese

Remove mushroom stems; chop and set aside. Rub mushroom caps lightly with olive oil. Combine chopped stems, onion, tarragon, pepper and bread crumbs; mix well. Toss with Swiss cheese and just enough milk to moisten. Stuff caps with mixture; sprinkle with Parmesan cheese and arrange on a baking sheet. Bake at 375 degrees for 15 minutes. Serves 6.

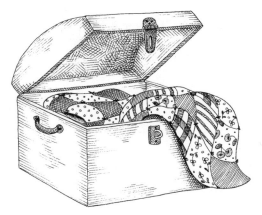

A memory quilt is sure to be a sweet reminder...transfer favorite pictures, handwritten recipes, invitations and birth announcements onto fabric squares. Stitch each together, then have everyone in the family sign and date the quilt.

Sweet Onion Dip

*Niccole Cera
Snellville, GA*

Serve this warm and bubbly from the oven with crispy crackers or breadsticks.

2 c. sweet onions, chopped
2 c. mayonnaise

2 c. Swiss cheese, grated

Mix ingredients together; pour into an 8"x8" baking dish. Bake at 350 degrees for 30 minutes or until golden. Makes about 6 cups.

Pecan-Olive Spread

*Kristie Rigo
Friedens, PA*

Spread on toasted bagels for a light lunch.

8-oz. pkg. cream cheese, softened
1/2 c. mayonnaise
1/8 t. hot pepper sauce

1/2 c. chopped pecans
1 c. green olives, chopped, liquid reserved

Combine cream cheese, mayonnaise, hot pepper sauce, pecans and olives together. Add 3 tablespoons reserved liquid from olives and mix well; chill before serving. Makes 3 cups.

*It is the sweet, simple things of life which are the real ones after all.
-Laura Ingalls Wilder*

Apricot Wraps

Claire Bertram
Lexington, KY

A favorite appetizer for our family no matter what the occasion...crunchy, sweet and so yummy!

14-oz. pkg. dried apricots
3/4 c. whole almonds
1 lb. bacon

1/3 c. plum jelly
2 T. soy sauce
1 t. ground ginger

Wrap each apricot around an almond. Cut bacon strips into thirds widthwise; wrap a strip around each apricot and secure with a toothpick. Place on 2 ungreased 15"x10" baking sheets; bake at 375 degrees for 25 minutes, turning once. In a small saucepan, combine jelly, soy sauce and ginger; cook over low heat for 5 minutes or until warm and smooth. Drain apricots on paper towels then arrange on serving platter; serve with sauce for dipping. Makes 4-1/2 dozen.

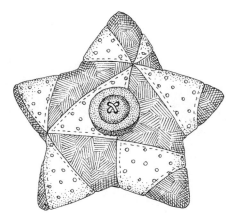

Vintage table linens and quilt squares make pretty trims for open cupboard shelves and are easily secured with decorative upholstery tacks.

Spicy Honey Chicken Wings

Karla Harrington
Anchorage, AK

Zesty and sweet...a sure winner!

1/2 c. chili sauce
1 T. honey
1 T. soy sauce

1/2 t. dry mustard
1/4 t. cayenne pepper
2 to 3 lbs. chicken wings

Combine first 5 ingredients in a 3-quart baking dish. Add chicken wings and toss to coat; cover and refrigerate one hour. Uncover dish and bake at 350 degrees for 45 to 60 minutes or until done. Serves 8.

Don't toss an old quilt just because it's worn. Stitch the prettiest pieces into a pincushion...a treasured keepsake.

Vanilla-Glazed Pumpkin Bread

Crystal Gwynn
Parkersburg, WV

There's nothing like the spicy scent of pumpkin bread baking in the oven...enjoy this with a glass of cold milk.

3 c. sugar
4 eggs, beaten
16-oz. can pumpkin
3-1/2 c. all-purpose flour
2 t. salt
1/2 t. cinnamon
1 t. baking powder

2 t. baking soda
1 t. nutmeg
1 c. oil
2/3 c. water
3 t. vanilla extract
1 c. chopped pecans

Beat sugar and eggs until fluffy; add pumpkin and mix well. In another bowl, combine flour, salt, cinnamon, baking powder, baking soda and nutmeg together. Stir dry ingredients into sugar mixture alternating with oil and water; add vanilla, mixing well. Beat for 3 minutes; fold in nuts. Divide and pour into 3 greased 5"x3" loaf pans. Bake at 350 degrees for one hour; brush hot glaze over tops of warm loaves. Makes 3 loaves.

Glaze:

1/2 c. sugar
1/4 c. water

1 t. vanilla extract

Mix ingredients together in a saucepan and boil for 3 minutes.

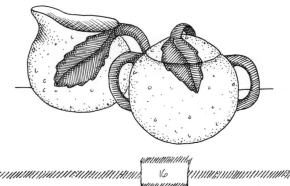

Chilled Vanilla Coffee

Cori Ritter
Port Washington, WI

For a special treat, serve in frosty glasses.

2 T. instant coffee granules
3/4 c. warm water
14-oz. can sweetened condensed
   milk

1 t. vanilla extract
4 c. ice cubes

Dissolve coffee in water; blend in condensed milk and vanilla.
Pour mixture into a blender and gradually add ice cubes; blend until
smooth. Serve immediately. Makes 4 servings.

Quilt sandwiches! Spread a favorite sandwich filling on
different types of bread...white, rye, pumpernickel and
sourdough. Slice each sandwich into quarters, then mix
& match each quarter on a serving plate.

Fabulous French Bread

Diana Krol
Nickerson, KS

Try slices dipped in warm marina sauce...delicious!

1 loaf French bread
1/2 c. butter, softened
2-1/4 oz. can sliced black olives
one bunch green onions,
    chopped

1/4 t. garlic powder
1 c. mayonnaise
2 hot peppers, chopped
1 c. shredded Cheddar cheese

Slice bread lengthwise; place cut sides up on an ungreased baking sheet. Combine the remaining ingredients; spread over bread slices. Bake at 350 degrees for 5 to 6 minutes or until the cheese is melted. Slice and serve while warm. Makes 12 servings.

Add a few mint sprigs or chamomile flower petals to a canister of tea...it will add a sweet aroma and mild flavor.

Fresh Tarragon Dip

Michele Bardwell
Bethel, CT

Bite-size pieces of pumpernickel or swirled rye bread are tasty with this fresh herbal dip...it won't last long!

3-oz. pkg. cream cheese,
   softened
2 T. sour cream

2 T. fresh tarragon, chopped
1 t. garlic, chopped

Blend all ingredients together until smooth; pack into a small crock and chill. Store refrigerated. Makes 1/2 cup.

If you plan for a year, plant a seed. If for ten years, plant a tree. If for one hundred years, make a quilt.
-Unknown

Hawaiian Fruit Dip

Shannon Smith
Berwick, PA

For a clever serving dish, slice a cantaloupe in half, scoop out the seeds and spoon in fruit dip.

1/2 c. sour cream
1 c. milk
3-1/2 oz. pkg. instant vanilla
    pudding

8-oz. can crushed pineapple
1/3 c. flaked coconut

Combine sour cream, milk and pudding in a small mixing bowl; blend until smooth. Add pineapple and coconut; mix thoroughly. Refrigerate for 30 minutes before serving. Makes 2-1/2 cups.

Make those you meet feel like an angel has kissed them,
and leave behind gentle memories when you go.
-Lynn Ray

Old-Fashioned Pink Soda

Kay Marone
Des Moines, IA

My girlfriends and I enjoy these on hot summer days...it makes us feel like kids again!

2 T. strawberries, crushed
2 T. crushed pineapple

1 c. plus 2 T. vanilla ice cream
1/3 c. strawberry soda, chilled

In a tall glass, combine strawberries, pineapple and 2 tablespoons ice cream; stir in soda. Add additional remaining ice cream until glass is almost full; pour in additional soda until glass is full. One serving.

Strawberry Smoothie

Amy Kasten
Oconomowoc, WI

A quick & easy treat!

20-oz. pkg. frozen strawberries
1 banana, sliced
8-oz. container mixed berry
   yogurt

1 c. milk
2 T. sugar
ice cubes

Combine ingredients in a blender; fill to the top with ice cubes. Blend until smooth. Makes 4 servings.

Artichoke-Spinach Dip

Jennifer Licon-Conner
Gooseberry Patch

Artichokes give a new twist to an old favorite.

6-oz. jar chopped artichoke
   hearts
1/2 c. frozen chopped spinach,
   thawed
8-oz. pkg. cream cheese,
   softened and warmed

1/2 c. Parmesan cheese, grated
1/2 t. crushed red pepper flakes
1/4 t. salt
1/8 t. garlic powder
1/8 t. pepper

Boil artichoke hearts and spinach in one cup of water in a saucepan over medium heat until artichoke hearts are tender; drain. Add artichoke heart mixture to warmed cream cheese; mix well. Blend in remaining ingredients. Makes about 3 cups.

Having a Sweet 16 slumber party for your daughter? Let the girls decorate their own fabric squares with paint, buttons and rick-rack, then stitch the squares together to create a special memory quilt.

Spring Onion Roll-Ups

Donna West
Spring Creek, NV

A tasty and oh-so simple appetizer.

1 bunch green onions
3-oz. pkg. cream cheese,
    softened

1/2 lb. cooked ham, thinly sliced

Rinse onions; trim to 6 or 7 inches long. Lay a slice of ham flat and spread with cream cheese. Place onion along one edge of ham; roll it up. Repeat with remaining ingredients; keep refrigerated until serving. Makes about 8 servings.

Pimento Cheese Spread

Angela Nichols
Mt. Airy, NC

Tastier than anything store-bought!

2 lbs. pasteurized process cheese
    spread
3 4-oz. jars chopped pimento

8-oz. pkg. cream cheese,
    softened
1 c. mayonnaise

Combine all ingredients; pack into a crock and refrigerate. Serve with crackers or spread on slices of homemade bread.

Strawberry-Orange Shakes

Vickie

So cool and refreshing!

2 c. orange juice
1/2 c. milk
10-oz. pkg. frozen sliced straw-
    berries, partially thawed
1-1/2 t. sugar

4 to 6 ice cubes
Garnish: whole strawberries,
    orange wedges or mint
    sprigs

Blend together orange juice, milk, strawberries and sugar until smooth;
add ice cubes blending again until smooth. Pour into glasses; garnish
with a whole strawberry, orange wedge or mint sprig. Serve
immediately. Makes 4 servings.

Recipes are traditions, not just random words of ingredients.
-Unknown

Daffodil Banana Crush Punch

Christi Perry
Gainesville, TX

My grandmother sent me off to college with this recipe...it was always a hit at every gathering!

6 c. water
4 c. sugar
32-oz. can pineapple juice
6-oz. can frozen orange juice
    concentrate, thawed

1/2 c. lemon juice
6 bananas, mashed
3 qts. ginger ale, chilled

Combine all ingredients except ginger ale; mix well. Divide into 8 plastic zipping freezer bags; freeze. Remove bags from freezer 3 to 4 hours before serving. Pour into punch bowl; add 3 quarts of chilled ginger ale. Makes 40 servings.

Pretty name tags let everyone know what beverages are being served. Cut out card stock using whimsical, decorative-edge scissors, then tie on with raffia or colorful rick-rack!

Fresh Fruit Salsa

Ruth Veazey
San Antonio, TX

Such a fresh taste...friends will love it!

2 apples, cored, peeled and diced
2 kiwi, peeled and diced
1 c. strawberries, sliced
1/2 c. orange juice
zest of one orange

2 T. brown sugar, packed
2 T. apple jelly
10-1/2 oz. pkg. flour tortillas,
   cut into triangles
sugar and cinnamon to taste

Combine apples, kiwi, strawberries, orange juice, zest, brown sugar and apple jelly together; cover and refrigerate. Sprinkle sugar and cinnamon over the tortillas; place on an ungreased baking sheet. Bake at 325 until warmed; remove from oven and let cool. Serve with salsa. Makes 5 cups.

Give new bits of fabric the illusion of age... set fabric in a large bowl and pour warm tea or coffee over it. Keep checking until the fabric takes on a vintage shade. Let dry, then iron. Frame the "aged" fabric with lots of sentimental photos or a handwritten recipe card.

Creamy Vanilla Dip

Eileen Popiel
Brunswick, OH

Enjoy spooned over slices of pound cake or fruit.

3-1/2 oz. pkg. instant vanilla
    pudding
1 c. milk

1 c. sour cream
8-oz. container whipped topping

Blend all ingredients together; makes about 2-1/2 cups.

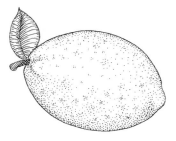

Chocolate-Dipped Fruit

Leslie Stimel
Gooseberry Patch

Also delicious with mandarin oranges, bananas or kiwi.

2 1-oz. sqs. semi-sweet
    chocolate

1 T. shortening
strawberries and grapes

Melt chocolate and shortening in a small saucepan over low heat.
Remove from heat and cool slightly. Dip fruit in chocolate until
partially coated, then lay on a wax paper-covered wire rack and
refrigerate until set, about 15 minutes.

Crunchy Macadamia Spread

Jo Ann

A dip with a little kick...horseradish!

8-oz. pkg. cream cheese,
    softened
2 T. milk
1/2 c. sour cream
2-1/2 t. prepared horseradish
1/4 c. green pepper, diced

1 green onion, chopped
1 t. garlic salt
1/4 t. pepper
1/2 c. chopped macadamia nuts
2 t. butter

Blend cream cheese and milk until smooth in a medium mixing bowl; stir in sour cream, horseradish, green pepper, onion, garlic salt and pepper. Spoon into an ungreased, shallow, 2-cup baking dish; set aside. Sauté nuts in a saucepan with butter for 3 to 4 minutes or until lightly browned; sprinkle over cream cheese mixture. Bake, uncovered, at 350 degrees for 20 minutes. Serve with a variety of crackers. Makes 2 cups.

Laughter is an instant vacation!
-Milton Berle

Yummy BLT Dip

Susan Curtis
Greenlawn, NY

So yummy spread on sourdough bread slices!

16-oz. carton sour cream
1 lb. bacon, crisply cooked and
   crumbled
1-1/2 t. onion salt

1/2 c. shredded Cheddar cheese
1 tomato, chopped and divided
1 c. lettuce, shredded

Combine sour cream, bacon and onion salt; spoon into a 9" pie plate. Top with cheese, 3/4 cup tomatoes, lettuce and then the remaining tomatoes; refrigerate. Makes about 3-1/2 cups.

Don't be shy! Enter a handmade quilt in the county fair...you just might be surprised how well you do!

Sweet Pumpkin Spread

Kathy Robinson
Marlton, NJ

Serve with apple slices for dipping or spread over toasted cinnamon bread or biscuits.

8-oz. cream cheese, softened
3/4 c. canned pumpkin
1/4 c. sweetened condensed
    milk
1 t. vanilla extract

1/2 t. cinnamon or pumpkin pie
    spice
1/2 c. finely chopped pecans
Garnish: maple syrup

Beat cream cheese in a medium mixing bowl until creamy and smooth; add pumpkin, milk, vanilla and spices, mixing well. Stir in pecans. Spoon into a serving bowl or small hollowed-out pumpkin; chill and drizzle top with maple syrup, if desired. Makes 2 cups.

Search tag sales for old bottles in colorful amber, cobalt or amethyst...perfect for holding freshly picked blossoms.

Crispy Peanut Butter Treats

Marilyn Kent
Clontarf, MN

The first recipe my daughter could easily make at
8 years-old...simple but really good!

1 c. creamy peanut butter
3 c. powdered sugar, divided
1/4 c. plus 2 T. butter, softened
  and divided

2 c. crispy rice cereal
3 T. milk
1 c. flaked coconut

Thoroughly mix together peanut butter, one cup powdered sugar and
2 tablespoons butter; stir in cereal. Form mixture into 3-inch logs;
chill. Mix the remaining powdered sugar and butter with milk in a
separate mixing bowl; dip one end of log into the frosting mixture. Roll
in coconut; chill. Makes 2 to 3 dozen.

White Hot Chocolate

Deanna Mann
Dudleyville, AZ

So creamy and comforting.

3 c. half-and-half, divided
2/3 c. vanilla chips
3-inch cinnamon stick

1/8 t. nutmeg
1 t. vanilla extract
Garnish: cinnamon

In a saucepan, combine 1/4 cup half-and-half, vanilla chips, cinnamon
stick and nutmeg. Stir over low heat until chips are melted; discard
cinnamon stick. Add remaining half-and-half; stir until warm. Remove
from heat and add vanilla. Pour into mugs; sprinkle with cinnamon, if
desired. Makes 4 servings.

Sauerkraut Balls

Sheila Gwaltney
Johnson City, TN

*Give these a try...I've served these to people who say they
don't like sauerkraut and they love them!*

1/3 c. onion, chopped
1 c. margarine
2 c. all-purpose flour, divided
2-1/2 c. milk, divided
2 lbs. ground beef, browned
1 T. prepared horseradish
1 T. Worcestershire sauce

1-1/2 t. dry mustard
2 drops hot pepper sauce
salt and pepper to taste
1 lb. sauerkraut, drained
1 egg
oil for deep frying
1 c. bread crumbs

Sauté onion in margarine. Stir in one cup flour; cook one minute and
blend in 1-1/2 cups milk. Stir to keep smooth and cook for one minute
more; remove from heat and set aside. Combine ground beef,
horseradish, Worcestershire sauce, mustard, hot pepper sauce, salt and
pepper; cook for 3 minutes. Remove from heat; mix in sauerkraut.
Pour in cream sauce; stir and chill at least 4 hours or overnight. Shape
into walnut-size balls and roll in remaining flour. Combine egg and
remaining milk; dip sauerkraut balls. Finally, coat with bread crumbs.
Deep-fry in 375 degree oil until done. Drain on paper towels. Makes
4 to 5 dozen.

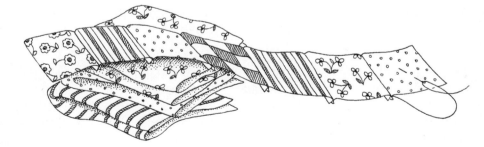

*Golf tees, glued upside down inside a wooden box, are just
right for organizing and holding spools of thread in place!*

9-Layer Mexicali Dip

Wendy Lee Paffenroth
Pine Island, NY

For a bolder taste, toss on hot pepper cheese and green chilies!

16-oz. can refried beans,
   warmed
3/4 c. lettuce, shredded
1 c. salsa
1 c. tortilla chips, crushed

1 c. sour cream
1 c. tomatoes, chopped
1/2 c. green peppers, chopped
1/2 c. sliced black olives
1 c. shredded taco cheese

Spread and layer ingredients in order listed on a large serving platter.
Serves 8.

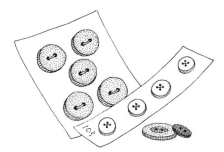

Horseradish Sauce

Connie Hilty
Pearland, TX

Try this in place of mayonnaise for your favorite recipes.

1 c. whipping cream, chilled
2-inch fresh horseradish root,
   grated

3 t. lemon juice
1/4 c. fresh chives, minced
salt and pepper to taste

Beat cream in deep bowl with electric mixer at medium speed until
thick, about 2 minutes. Whisk in remaining ingredients until just
combined. Keep chilled up to 2 hours; whisk briefly before serving.
Makes about 2 cups.

Cheddar Quick Bread

Lori Burris
Gooseberry Patch

Homemade bread...without spending hours in the kitchen.

3-1/2 c. biscuit baking mix
2-1/2 c. shredded sharp Cheddar
   cheese
1 t. garlic salt

1/3 c. fresh chives, chopped
2 eggs
1-1/4 c. milk

Combine biscuit mix, cheese, garlic salt and chives in a large mixing bowl; set aside. Beat eggs and milk together in another mixing bowl; stir into cheese mixture until just moistened. Pour into 4 greased and floured 5"x3" loaf pans; bake at 350 degrees for 35 to 40 minutes. Cool for 10 minutes; remove from pans. Slice and serve warm. Makes 4 mini loaves.

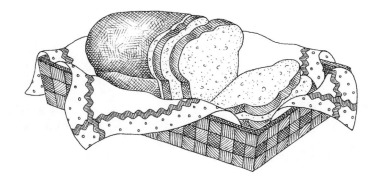

Friends are like pillars on a porch. Sometimes they hold you up, sometimes they lean on you, and sometimes it's just enough to know they are standing by.
-Unknown

Brown Sugar Bites

Amy Magnuson
Palmer, AK

This always seems to be everyone's favorite snack to nibble on when friends get together.

1 T. cornstarch
1/2 c. brown sugar, packed
1/3 c. vinegar
6 T. pineapple juice

2 t. soy sauce
4 20-oz. pkgs. mini sausage
   links

Bring cornstarch, brown sugar, vinegar, pineapple juice and soy sauce to a boil in a small saucepan; pour over sausages. Heat in a slow cooker or heavy saucepan until warmed. Makes 20 servings.

Apple-Sausages

Amanda Zuech
Franklinville, NY

This disappears as soon as it hits the table!

1 lb. Polish sausage, sliced   1 qt. apple juice

Heat sausages and apple juice in a saucepan over high heat until juice is almost completely cooked down, stirring often. Serves 4 to 6.

Anise Toast

Virginia Arbisi
Elmont, NY

Spread with butter for a truly old-fashioned treat.

2 eggs
2/3 c. sugar

1 t. anise seed
1 c. all-purpose flour

Beat eggs until thick; add sugar, beating until fluffy. Blend in anise seed; gradually add flour and mix well. Pour into a greased and floured 9"x5" loaf pan; bake at 375 degrees for 20 minutes or until cake tester inserted in center comes out clean. Pan will only appear 1/4 full. Cool on a rack for 5 minutes, then cut into 1/2-inch thick slices. Lay slices on a baking sheet and lightly toast both sides under the broiler. Serve warm. Makes about 18 slices.

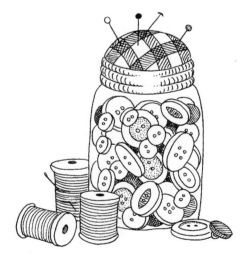

If your favorite cookbook is a little worn, give it a fresh look by covering it with cheery gingham edged in rick-rack!

Honey-Grapefruit Granita

Tiffany Brinkley
Broomfield, CO

So refreshing!

2-1/4 c. sugar
2 c. water

4 c. pink grapefruit juice
1/3 c. honey, warmed

Combine sugar and water in a large saucepan; bring to a boil. Boil until sugar dissolves, stirring constantly; cool. Combine sugar mixture with grapefruit juice; stir. Add warmed honey to juice; stir well. Pour into a 13"x9" baking dish; cover and freeze at least 8 hours or until firm. Use the tines of a fork to make mixture fluffy; spoon mixture into glasses. Makes 6 cups.

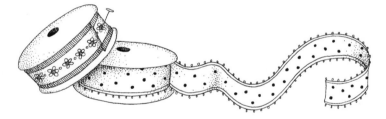

Lemon Velvet Smoothie

Debbie Stulc
Spokane, WA

Pretty garnished with red raspberries.

8-oz. carton lemon yogurt
6-oz. can frozen orange concen-
    trate

2-1/2 c. milk
1 t. vanilla extract

Combine all ingredients in a blender and blend thoroughly. Makes 4 servings.

Water Chestnut Roll-Ups

Cheri Branca
Victor, NY

Crunchy water chestnuts covered with a sugary glaze...yummy!

1 lb. bacon
8-oz. can whole water chestnuts

1/3 c. catsup
1/2 c. sugar

Cut bacon in half, widthwise; roll one piece of bacon around one whole water chestnut. Place with the cut side down in a 13"x9" baking dish; bake at 350 degrees for one hour and drain. Combine catsup and sugar together; pour over chestnuts and bake for one more hour. Remove to a serving platter; serve with a toothpick in each. Makes about 32 servings.

An antique fruit crate with handles makes a terrific serving tray for cold summer drinks. Give it a little lift by painting or stenciling on some bright red cherries.

Garden Club Luncheon

Flowerpot Cheese Appetizers

Michelle Campen
Peoria, IL

Guests will be impressed with the clever serving dishes!

8-oz. pkg. cream cheese,
    softened
1 c. ricotta cheese
1/2 c. Monterey Jack cheese,
    shredded
1 clove garlic, minced

1/2 c. fresh parsley, chopped and
    divided
1/8 t. salt
1/4 t. pepper
1/4 c. fresh chives, chopped

Blend cheeses, garlic, 1/4 cup parsley, salt and pepper together until smooth; cover and chill at least one hour. Just before serving, line four new 3-inch flowerpots with plastic wrap and spoon cheese mixture into each, filling to the brim. Sprinkle with remaining parsley and chives. Serve with crackers. Makes about 2-1/2 cups.

Sew brightly colored buttons on a 6-inch length of elastic, overlapping each slightly, then stitch the ends together...pretty button napkin rings!

Zesty Black Bean Salsa

Lynn Simone
Smithfield, VA

If you have a vegetable garden take advantage of the crisp vegetables on hand. Just remember that fresh corn will need to be boiled first, then cut from the cob before adding to this recipe.

15-1/2 oz. can black beans, rinsed and drained
15-1/4 oz. can corn, drained
3/4 c. red pepper, diced
1/2 c. green onion, sliced

1/3 c. cilantro, chopped
1/4 c. lime juice
2 t. cumin
1/4 t. garlic salt

Combine beans, corn, red pepper, onion and cilantro in a large mixing bowl; mix well. Whisk together lime juice, cumin and garlic salt together in a separate bowl; pour over bean mixture and toss gently. Serve with tortilla chips. Makes 4 cups.

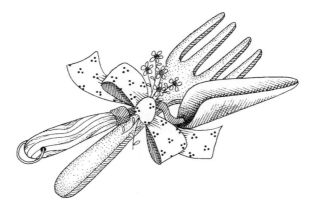

When I last took the time to look into the heart of a flower, it opened up a whole new world; a world where every country walk would be an adventure, where every garden would become an enchanted one.
-Princess Grace of Monaco

Herbal Cheese Spread

*Chris White
Harlingen, TX*

I love this best when spread on warm toasty baguette slices.

8-oz. pkg. cream cheese,
   softened
1 T. fresh rosemary, chopped
1 T. fresh oregano, chopped
1 T. fresh thyme, chopped
1 T. fresh basil, chopped

1 T. fresh parsley, chopped
1 T. fresh chives, chopped
1 T. lemon juice
1/2 t. Worcestershire sauce
1/2 t. dry mustard

Combine all ingredients together; refrigerate. Bring to room temperature to serve; makes about 1-1/4 cups.

Set a large birdhouse in the middle of a vintage wheelbarrow, then surround it with potting soil and cascading flowers. What a beautiful addition to your garden or patio.

BLT Bites

Deanna Smith
Huntington, WV

A favorite sandwich becomes an appetizer!

16 to 20 cherry tomatoes
8 slices bacon, crisply cooked
   and crumbled
1/2 c. mayonnaise

1/3 c. green onion, chopped
3 T. Parmesan cheese, grated
2 T. fresh parsley, finely chopped

Cut a thin slice off the top of each tomato; scoop out and discard pulp. Invert tomatoes on a paper towel to drain. Combine the remaining ingredients in a small mixing bowl; mix well. Spoon mixture into each tomato; refrigerate for several hours before serving. Serves 6.

Make a sunflower playhouse; just plant giant sunflower seeds in a large circle. What a great place for the kids to spend their summer days!

Hot Chicken Salad

Brenda Doak
Gooseberry Patch

If you don't care for almonds, use water chestnuts for crunch!

1 c. rice, cooked
1 c. cooked chicken, diced
1 c. celery, chopped
10-3/4 oz. can cream of chicken
    soup
3/4 c. mayonnaise

3/4 c. slivered almonds
2 T. onion, chopped
1 c. corn flake cereal, coarsely
    crushed
2 T. butter

Combine all ingredients except the corn cereal and butter; place in an
8"x8" greased baking dish. Top with crushed cereal; dot with butter.
Bake at 350 degrees for 45 minutes. Makes 4 servings.

Create a children's garden using plants with animal
names...lamb's ear, hens & chicks, foxglove, tiger lilies.
What fun for them to take care of their "animals!"

Garlic & Vegetable Pasta

Nancy Brown
St. Louis, MO

Use any favorite vegetables...this is a winner!

2-1/2 T. olive oil
1/2 clove garlic, pressed
12 baby carrots
1 potato, chopped
8 mushrooms, sliced

1/2 c. spinach, cooked and
 drained
1/2 c. rotini, cooked and drained
Garnish: Parmesan cheese

Heat oil in a non-stick skillet. Add garlic, carrots and potato; cover and cook over low heat 10 minutes. Add in mushrooms and sauté until tender. Stir in spinach and rotini; mix well. Remove from heat; pour into serving dish and sprinkle with Parmesan cheese. Makes 2 to 3 servings.

Create garden placecards! Write guests' names on plant markers and tuck each in a small clay pot along with seed packets, garden gloves and a trowel.

Fresh Tomato Pie

Roxanne Bixby
W. Franklin, NH

Slice and serve with fresh fruit for a deliciously light lunch.

2 c. buttermilk biscuit baking
   mix
2/3 c. milk
3 tomatoes, peeled and thinly
   sliced

salt and pepper to taste
2 t. fresh chives
2 t. fresh basil
1 c. mayonnaise
1 c. Cheddar cheese, grated

Combine biscuit mix with milk to form dough; pat into a greased 9" pie plate. Layer tomato slices; sprinkle on salt, pepper, chives and basil. Mix mayonnaise and cheese together in a separate mixing bowl; spread over the tomato slices. Bake at 375 degrees for 40 minutes or until cheese crust is golden. Makes 8 servings.

*It's difficult to think anything but pleasant thoughts
while eating a homegrown tomato.
-Lewis Grizzard*

Ham & Egg Cups

Kristi Holtz
Scotia, NY

For a different taste try slices of maple or brown sugar ham.

4 slices deli ham
2 c. shredded Cheddar cheese,
　　divided
4 t. onion, chopped and divided

6 eggs, beaten
1/4 c. cottage cheese
salt and pepper to taste

Coat 4 ramekins or custard cups with non-stick vegetable spray and place one slice of ham in the bottom of each. Sprinkle with 1/4 cup Cheddar cheese and one teaspoon onion; set aside. Mix eggs, cottage cheese, salt and pepper in a mixing bowl until well blended; divide and pour into the ham cups. Top with remaining cheese; bake at 350 degrees for 25 to 30 minutes or until a knife inserted comes out clean. Serves 4.

If I had a single flower for every time I think about you,
I could walk forever in my garden.
-Claudia A. Grandi

Cheesy Eggplant Patties

Helen Hellriegel
South Plainfield, NJ

This recipe is from a sweet friend who shared many of her best recipes with me.

1 eggplant, peeled and cubed
1-1/4 c. cracker or bread crumbs
1-1/4 c. shredded sharp Cheddar
    cheese
2 eggs, beaten

2 T. onion, diced
1/2 t. garlic powder
1/2 t. salt
1/8 t. pepper
2 T. oil

Place eggplant in a saucepan; cover with water. Bring to a boil; simmer until eggplant is tender. Mash eggplant; stir in crumbs, cheese, eggs, onion, garlic powder, salt and pepper. Shape into 3-inch round patties; fry in heated oil for about 3 minutes on each side or until golden brown. Makes 2 dozen.

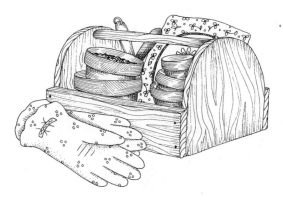

Blooms from edible flowers such as pansy, impatiens or nasturtium flowers are so pretty frozen in ice cubes. Place the ice cubes in a large clay pot, then nestle in a ramekin or crock of dip...what a lovely way to keep it chilled for guests!

Vegetable Garden Soup

Lynda McCormick
Burkburnett, TX

Plan ahead when preparing this tasty soup...it should sit overnight to allow all the flavors to blend.

2 T. olive oil
1 onion, finely chopped
2 leeks, chopped
2 potatoes, peeled and diced
2 white turnips, peeled and diced
3 carrots, peeled and sliced
3 stalks celery, diced

1/2 lb. sliced mushrooms
8 c. hot water
2 cubes vegetable bouillon
1 t. paprika
1 t. cumin
2 c. frozen peas, thawed
salt and pepper to taste

Heat oil in a heavy soup pan; sauté onion and leeks over medium heat until tender, about 10 minutes. Add potatoes, turnips, carrots, celery, mushrooms, water, bouillon, paprika and cumin; bring to a boil. Reduce heat; cover and simmer for 45 minutes or until vegetables are tender. Add peas and season with salt and pepper. Refrigerate for several hours or overnight to blend flavors; reheat when ready to serve. Makes 8 to 10 servings.

Fresh garden vegetables make the best broth and it's so easy! Just add chopped carrots or cabbage to a pot of boiling water and simmer 30 minutes. Cool, then freeze in ice cube trays until ready to use.

Dilly Cucumber Squares

Carolyn Oland
Frederick, MD

What could be better? Easy to make and always a hit!

8-oz. pkg. cream cheese,
   softened
1/4 c. mayonnaise
1.05-oz. pkg. Italian dressing
   mix

1 loaf sliced party rye bread
1 cucumber, thinly sliced
Garnish: fresh dill, chopped

Blend cream cheese and mayonnaise together until smooth; stir in Italian dressing mix. Spread on slices of bread; top with a cucumber slice and sprinkling of dill. Cover with paper towel and refrigerate overnight. Makes about 24 servings.

Italian Seasoning

Kay Marone
Des Moines, IA

Sprinkle on pasta, sandwiches, roasted potatoes, garlic bread...anywhere you'd like a little extra flavor.

2 T. dried basil
2 T. dried marjoram
2 T. dried oregano
2 T. dried coriander

2 T. dried thyme
2 T. dried rosemary
2 T. dried savory
1 t. hot red pepper flakes

Combine all ingredients in a food processor until finely ground. Transfer to a tightly sealed container. Store in a cool dark place for up to 3 months. Makes about one cup.

Celery Seed Dressing

Carol Burns
Gooseberry Patch

*This fresh dressing is hard to beat on a crisp, tossed salad...also
try this instead of mayonnaise in your other favorite recipes.*

2/3 c. sugar
1 t. salt
5 T. vinegar
1 T. lemon juice

1 t. dry mustard
1 t. onion juice
1/2 T. celery seed
1 c. oil

Blend all ingredients except the oil in a blender. When sugar is
dissolved, add oil and mix thoroughly. Makes about one cup.

*Trim a head of cabbage and cut a hole in the center just big
enough for a paper cup to fit inside. Fill the cup with water
and fresh flowers for a clever vase!*

Pineapple Chicken Salad

Teri Bottoms
Cantonment, FL

Scoop into hollowed-out tomatoes or melon halves.

3 to 4 boneless, skinless chicken
   breasts
2 stalks celery, chopped and
   divided
1 carrot, sliced
1/4 c. roasted mixed nuts,
   chopped

1/2 apple, cored, peeled and
   chopped
10 seedless grapes, halved
8-oz. carton pineapple yogurt

Boil chicken breasts with one stalk celery and carrot until juices run
clear when chicken is pierced. Discard celery and carrot; chop chicken
and set aside. Mix together remaining celery, nuts and apple; carefully
add grapes and toss. Combine chicken and yogurt together in
a separate mixing bowl; add nut mixture. Makes 6 to 8 servings.

Just for fun, stencil watermelons on painted metal tubs,
sap buckets and vintage jars. Filled with ice and
beverages, flowers or candles, they will add
an instant summertime feel!

Crunchy Asparagus & Pasta

Janet Pastrick
Gooseberry Patch

At our family reunions, we have exchanged many recipes over the years...this is my favorite!

5 cloves garlic, minced
2 t. crushed red pepper flakes
2 drops hot pepper sauce
1/4 c. oil
2 T. butter
1 lb. asparagus, chopped

salt and pepper to taste
1/2 t. celery seed
1/4 c. fresh Parmesan cheese,
   shredded
1/2 lb. elbow macaroni, cooked
   and drained

In a large skillet, sauté garlic, red pepper flakes and hot pepper sauce in oil and butter for 2 to 3 minutes. Add asparagus, salt, pepper and celery seed; sauté until asparagus is crisp-tender, about 8 to 10 minutes. Remove from heat; mix in Parmesan cheese. Pour over hot pasta; toss to coat. Makes 4 to 6 servings.

An old-fashioned mailbox placed on your garden gate makes a handy spot to store small garden tools, gloves and seed packets. Give it a coat of colorful paint for added whimsy!

Lemon Daisy

Michelle Campen
Peoria, IL

*Invite friends over, sit in the shade and enjoy catching
up with one another.*

1/2 c. grenadine syrup
1/3 c. freshly squeezed lemon
    juice

2 c. club soda
2 c. lemon-flavored soda
Garnish: lemon slices

Stir grenadine and lemon juice together; pour into 4 ice-filled goblets.
Top each goblet with 1/2 cup of each soda. Garnish with lemon slice.
Serves 4.

Refreshing Mint Punch

Mary Murray
Gooseberry Patch

I love this! It's such a nice change from traditional punch.

2 c. mint leaves, packed
2 c. water

12-oz. can frozen lemonade
1 qt. ginger ale

Bring mint and water to boil; bruise with potato masher. Set aside
overnight; strain and discard solids. Add lemonade, 3 lemonade cans
of water and ginger ale to mint mixture; mix well and serve. Makes
10 to 12 servings.

Tea Sandwiches

Jo Ann

Fresh herbs and feta cheese are a terrific sandwich combination.

1 c. butter, softened
8-oz. pkg. cream cheese,
   softened
1/2 c. crumbled feta cheese
1/2 c. fresh parsley, chopped
1 T. fresh basil, chopped

1 T. fresh tarragon, chopped
1 T. fresh rosemary, chopped
salt and pepper to taste
12 to 16 thin slices wheat or
   oatmeal bread

Combine all ingredients, except the bread, in a large mixing bowl; blend thoroughly. Spread desired amount of herb mixture over half of the bread slices; close sandwiches with remaining slices. Remove crusts; cut into desired shapes and chill for one hour. Makes about 6 to 8 sandwiches.

A portable herb garden! Tuck several herb plants inside a vintage tin picnic basket...so easy to carry to the kitchen when it's time to snip fresh herbs.

Creamy Onion-Potato Soup

Jennifer Niemi
Kingston, Nova Scotia

I don't know why, but we don't eat a lot of potatoes at our house. So when twenty-five pounds were brought home instead of five, I had to be a little creative in order to use them all. Twenty-five pounds later and I was satisfied with this recipe...it's tasty and delicious!

3 T. butter
5 c. onions, chopped
6 c. potatoes, cubed
4 c. vegetable broth
3 cloves garlic, chopped

1/4 t. pepper
1/2 t. celery seed
2-1/2 t. garlic salt
3 c. milk
1 carrot, grated

Melt butter in a 4-quart saucepan; sauté onions until soft. Add potatoes, vegetable broth, garlic, pepper, celery seed and garlic salt; bring to a boil. Reduce heat and simmer, covered, for 20 to 30 minutes or until potatoes are tender. Cool slightly and, working with small portions at a time, purée in a blender. Return to saucepan; add milk. Heat to desired temperature but do not allow to boil; stir in carrot before serving. Serves 6.

Give favorite homemade soups extra flavor by substituting one cup of stock for one cup of milk in the recipe.

Portabella Pasta

Elizabeth Thompson
Aberdeen, NJ

What could be easier? Toss a crisp salad to go alongside and enjoy!

1-1/2 oz. pkg. dried portabella
   mushrooms
3 T. oil
1 shallot, minced
1 sweet onion, chopped
1 bunch green onions, chopped
2 cloves garlic, minced
3 T. soy sauce

1/2 c . red wine
salt and pepper to taste
1 bunch parsley, chopped and
   divided
12-oz. pkg. bowtie pasta, cooked
   and drained
Garnish; fresh Parmesan cheese,
   grated

Fill a large glass bowl with water; add mushrooms, cover and soak
until softened, about 45 minutes. Strain mushrooms, reserving and
setting aside the liquid. Rinse mushrooms and coarsely chop. Heat oil;
sauté shallot, onions and garlic until soft. Add mushrooms; sauté
5 more minutes. Pour in soy sauce, red wine and reserved mushroom
liquid; continue to simmer until liquid is reduced to half. Salt and
pepper to taste; pour over pasta. Toss with remaining parsley; top with
grated cheese. Makes 4 servings.

*Wrap sandwiches for your garden party in wax paper and
tie with a length of gingham ribbon. Serve them in a
favorite basket lined with a vintage dishtowel.*

Ruby Punch

Sammy Polizzi-Morrison
Aurora, CO

*Enjoy a warm cup of this while taking an early
morning walk through the garden.*

2 32-oz. cans cranberry juice
46-oz. can unsweetened
   pineapple juice
1 c. brown sugar, packed
1/4 t. salt

4 t. whole cloves
6 cinnamon sticks, broken
6 whole allspice
6 cardamom
1 t. orange zest

Combine juices and brown sugar in a large saucepan; heat until sugar
dissolves. Place salt, cloves, cinnamon sticks, allspice, cardamom and
zest in cheesecloth; tie closed and immerse in juice. Simmer
15 minutes; remove spice bag before serving. Makes 18 servings.

*A garden journal is the perfect spot to keep photos of the
garden at each stage that it's in bloom. Then next year, it's
easy to see where new plants can be placed for extra color.*

Glazed Lemon Bread

Denise Pawlak
Grinnell, IA

Very moist...enjoy it warm from the oven.

3/4 c. shortening	1/4 t. baking soda
1-1/2 c. sugar	1/4 t. salt
3 eggs	3/4 c. buttermilk
2-1/4 c. all-purpose flour	zest of one lemon

Cream shortening and sugar; add eggs one at a time, beating well after each addition. In a separate mixing bowl, combine flour, baking soda and salt; add to sugar mixture. Stir in buttermilk and zest. Divide into two 9"x5" greased loaf pans; bake at 350 degrees for 30 to 35 minutes. Pour glaze over the tops while still warm. Makes 16 servings.

Glaze:

3/4 c. sugar   juice of one lemon

Stir together sugar and lemon juice until smooth.

Having friends over for tea? Scatter violets or pansies on the tablecloth...looks so cheery with your prettiest teacups.

Coffee Cake Crescents

Liz Marcellin
Newark, CA

Handed-down recipes are always special...this is my mother's.

1 pkg. active dry yeast
2 T. warm water
1 c. less 2 T. milk
4 c. all-purpose flour
1 c. butter or margarine
1 c. plus 1 T. sugar, divided

1 t. salt
3 eggs, separated
1 T. cinnamon
Optional: 1/2 c. finely chopped
   walnuts

Sprinkle yeast over warm water and add enough milk to make one cup; set aside. In a large mixing bowl, combine flour, butter, one tablespoon of sugar and salt; set aside. Beat 3 egg yolks; mix in with yeast mixture. Add yeast mixture to the flour mixture; blend well. Cover dough and chill in refrigerator overnight. Separate the dough into thirds; roll out each third into 1/4-inch thick rectangle; set aside. Beat 3 egg whites and the remaining sugar together; spread evenly over each rectangle. Sprinkle with cinnamon and chopped nuts, if desired. Shape into crescent shapes; place on baking sheets and let rise one hour, will not double in bulk. Bake at 325 degrees for 30 minutes or until golden brown. While baking, prepare frosting and frost while warm. Makes 3 large crescents.

Frosting:

1 c. powdered sugar
1 T. butter, softened

2 T. milk

Combine the ingredients and blend well, adjusting milk and powdered sugar to desired consistency.

Use wire soda crates to tote refreshments
to and from the garden...so easy!

Maple Bread Pudding

Joan Barton
Goffstown, NH

Nothing ends a meal like quite like old-fashioned bread pudding.

4 c. French bread, cubed
1 c. raisins
1/4 c. chopped pecans
4 eggs
1/2 c. sugar
1/8 t. nutmeg

2 c. milk
1/2 c. maple syrup
Garnish: whipped topping,
    maple syrup and pecan
    halves

Spread bread cubes in an 8"x8" greased baking dish; sprinkle with raisins and pecans. Beat eggs in a mixing bowl; add sugar, nutmeg, milk and syrup. Pour evenly over bread mixture; bake at 350 degrees for one hour or until knife inserted in center tests clean. To serve, spoon warm pudding into individual dessert bowls and top each with a dollop of whipped cream. Drizzle tops with maple syrup and sprinkle on pecan halves. Serves 6.

Old-Time Icebox Cookies

Rosalie Benson
Coats, NC

Way back when I was growing up and families had to rely on iceboxes, it was my job to empty the drip pan beneath the icebox each night...sometimes I forgot. If we heard grumbling when my father arose in the morning, I knew he'd made his way to the kitchen and stepped in overflow water on the kitchen floor!

1 c. butter or margarine
2 c. brown sugar, packed
2 eggs
3-1/2 c. all-purpose flour

1 t. baking soda
1/2 t. salt
1 c. chopped nuts

Cream butter and sugar together in a large mixing bowl. Add eggs, individually; beating well after each addition. In a separate mixing bowl, combine flour, baking soda and salt; add to the sugar mixture, mixing well. Fold in nuts; divide dough and roll into 2 logs. Wrap in wax paper; refrigerate overnight. Slice thinly and place on greased baking sheet; bake at 350 degrees for 7 to 10 minutes. Makes 4 dozen.

A morning glory at my window satisfies me more than the metaphysics of books.
-Walt Whitman

Meringue Kisses

Dorothy Glathart
Sheldon, IL

*Tuck a sweet surprise inside…add a chocolate
drop in the center of each meringue after placing on the
baking sheet, then gently spread meringue over to cover.*

7 egg whites, room temperature
1-1/2 c. sugar

1 t. vanilla extract
1 t. vinegar

Beat egg whites until stiff. Very gradually add sugar, vanilla and
vinegar; beating well. Drop onto an ungreased baking sheet; bake at
225 degrees for one hour; turn off oven but leave meringues in the
oven to dry for at least 6 hours or overnight. Do not open oven door
until hardened. Makes 3 dozen.

*A sap bucket is just the right size for an ice bucket. Filled
with ice and a new garden trowel, guests can
help themselves…fun!*

Nectarine Crisp

Kathy Warren
Gooseberry Patch

It's not necessary to peel the nectarines, so this is not only yummy, but easy to prepare, too.

1-2/3 c. sugar, divided
1/2 t. cinnamon
1/2 t. salt
1 T. cornstarch
1/3 c. water

4 c. nectarines, sliced
1/3 c. plus 1 T. chilled butter,
   divided
3/4 c. all-purpose flour
Garnish: whipped topping

Combine 2/3 cup sugar, cinnamon, salt and cornstarch in a saucepan; pour in water and boil for one minute. Place nectarine slices in a buttered 10"x6" baking pan; pour syrup over the top. Dot with one tablespoon butter and mix gently. Combine flour, remaining sugar and butter together in a separate bowl until mixture resembles coarse crumbs; sprinkle over fruit. Bake uncovered at 350 degrees for 40 minutes; serve with whipped topping, if desired. Serves 4 to 6.

CREAM

Bring a little of the garden inside...use an antique trellis to hold bath or hand towels.

Honey-Pecan Bars

Jackie Crough
Salina, KS

Chock full of things that are not only good, but good for you!

1-1/2 c. sesame seed
1 c. flaked coconut
1/2 c. sunflower seeds
1/2 c. chopped pecans

3/4 c. honey
1/4 c. powdered milk
1/2 t. vanilla extract

Toast sesame seed, coconut, sunflower seeds and pecans in an ungreased 11"x8" baking dish at 400 degrees for about 20 minutes; stir occasionally. Combine honey and powdered milk in a saucepan; bring to a boil. Remove from heat; add vanilla. Pour honey mixture over seeds; stir well and press together. Allow to cool; cut into bars and wrap individually in plastic wrap. Makes 18 bars.

Flowered handkerchiefs make such pretty valances...just lay over a spring rod on a window.

Melt-in-Your-Mouth Cookies

Bethany Zemaitis
Pittsburgh, PA

*Mom has made these cookies for years. True to their name,
they really do melt in your mouth!*

1/2 lb. butter	3/4 c. cornstarch
5-1/2 T. powdered sugar	1 c. all-purpose flour

Cream butter, powdered sugar and cornstarch together. Add flour and
mix well. Roll into balls or drop by teaspoonfuls onto a greased baking
sheet. Bake at 350 degrees for 20 minutes; when cool spread with
glaze. Makes 3 dozen.

Glaze:

3/4 c. powdered sugar	milk
1/2 t. banana flavoring	yellow food coloring

Mix powered sugar, flavoring and just enough milk to make glaze
spreadable. Add coloring to desired shade; spread onto cookies.

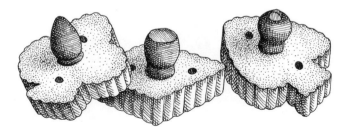

*The prettiest croutons...cut bread with a small cookie
cutter. Brush cut-outs with butter, place on a baking
sheet and bake at 350 degrees until golden.*

Golden Raisin Buns

Sharon Hoskins
Warrensburg, MO

When you need a little something sweet, these will hit the spot.

1 c. water
1/2 c. butter
1 t. sugar
1/4 t. salt

1 c. all-purpose flour
4 eggs
1/2 c. golden raisins

Bring water, butter, sugar and salt to a boil in a saucepan. Remove from heat; add flour, stirring until mixture pulls away from sides of pan. Add eggs one at a time, beating well after each addition. Stir in raisins. Drop by heaping tablespoonfuls onto an ungreased baking sheet; bake at 375 degrees for 30 minutes. Makes 2 dozen.

Apple-Pumpkin Butter

Sandy Dodson
Indianapolis, IN

Through the years I have tried to perfect apple butter recipes but they always seem to lack something special. I sincerely think this recipe is just right!

1-3/4 c. canned pumpkin
1 c. apple, peeled, cored and
   grated

1 c. apple juice
1/2 c. brown sugar, packed
3/4 t. pumpkin pie spice

Combine all ingredients in a medium saucepan; bring to a boil. Reduce heat to low; simmer for 1-1/2 hours, stirring occasionally. Makes 3 cups.

All of the flowers of tomorrow are in the seeds of today.
-Proverb

Strawberry-Pretzel Salad

Liz Hall
Worthington, IN

This salad disappears quickly...our family loves it!

2 c. pretzels, coarsely crushed
3/4 c. margarine, melted
1 c. plus 4 T. sugar, divided
8-oz. pkg. cream cheese,
   softened

8-oz. carton whipped topping
6-oz. pkg. strawberry gelatin
2 c. boiling water
2 10-oz. pkgs. frozen
   strawberries

Mix pretzels, margarine, and 4 tablespoons of sugar together. Spread into a 13"x9" pan and bake at 400 degrees for 6 minutes. Combine cream cheese and remaining sugar; fold in whipped topping and spread over cooled pretzel mixture. Dissolve gelatin in 2 cups of boiling water in a separate bowl; stir in strawberries until berries start to separate and gelatin starts to thicken. Pour over the cheese mixture; refrigerate until set. Serves 12.

Looking for a simple placecard idea? Write names on placecards and punch a hole in the corner, then simply slip over the stems of apples or pears!

Lemony Fruit Salad

Becky Sykes
Gooseberry Patch

Served in a jadite or blue milkglass bowl, this is one of those favorites that takes you back to Mom's kitchen.

1 Red Delicious apple, peeled, cored and chopped
1 Granny Smith apple, peeled cored and chopped
1 nectarine, pitted and sliced

2 stalks celery, chopped
1/2 c. dried cranberries
3/4 c. chopped walnuts
8-oz. carton lemon yogurt

Combine apples, nectarine, celery, cranberries and walnuts in a large bowl; stir in yogurt. Chill until ready to serve. Makes 6 servings.

Bundle together fresh herb cuttings from the garden with jute to make an herb basting brush. Dip the herb bundle in a mixture of olive oil and pressed garlic and use to baste meat or chicken as it's cooking on the grill.

Clothespin Cookies

Gloria Mulhern
Windham, OH

Tint the filling any color, pastels are really pretty, or just dip the ends in colored sugar.

1 lb. butter, softened
24-oz. carton small curd cottage
   cheese
1/2 t. salt

4 c. all-purpose flour
30 to 60 rounded clothespins
Garnish: powdered sugar

Combine butter, cottage cheese and salt in a large mixing bowl and mix well. Add flour in 1/2-cup increments until incorporated; dough will be thick and sticky. Using an equal mixture of sugar and flour on the rolling surface; divide dough into 4 equal parts and roll out into a rectangle 1/8-inch thick. Cut dough into 5"x2" rectangles, then diagonally cut each to form 2 triangles. Roll each triangle around a dry clothespin, wide end first, to form a crescent-like roll. Lay on a lightly greased baking sheet with point of crescent facing up. Dough will not spread; do not let crescents touch. Bake at 350 degrees for 15 to 20 minutes, until dough is set and bottoms are light brown. Slide off clothespins while still warm. Cool and fill with creme filling. Dust with powdered sugar before serving. Makes 12 to 14 dozen.

Cream Filling:

4 t. meringue powder
4 T. water
1 c. butter, softened
1 c. shortening

2 t. vanilla extract
4 c. powdered sugar
1 c. half-and-half, warm

Blend meringue powder and water together; add butter, shortening, and vanilla, blending well. Add sugar slowly, mixing well until smooth. Pour in half-and-half; beat 5 to 8 minutes until very creamy and light. Use a pastry bag to pipe filling into cooled shells.

Garden Club Luncheon

Mother's Tea Cakes

Phyllis Peters
Three Rivers, MI

*This recipe was shared with me over 20 years ago...simple
and old-fashioned, but oh-so good.*

3/4 c. shortening
2 c. sugar
3 eggs
3-1/2 c. all-purpose flour
1 t. salt

2 t. baking powder
1 t. baking soda
1/2 c. buttermilk
1 t. vanilla extract

Cream shortening and sugar together; add one egg at a time, beating
well after each addition. Combine flour, salt, baking powder and
baking soda; stir into sugar mixture alternating with buttermilk. Add
vanilla. Roll out onto a floured surface to 1/4-inch thickness. Cut out
shapes with cookie cutter. Bake at 400 degrees for 10 minutes or until
done. Makes 2 dozen.

Warm cookies and milk are good for you.
-Robert Fulghum

Strawberry Shortcake

Jen Sell
Farmington, MN

This is absolutely the best shortcake I've ever tasted! My best friend, Shelly, and I go berry picking together and can hardly wait to get home to make this. Everyone will ask for seconds...be prepared, you may want to make two!

1 c. all-purpose flour
1 t. baking powder
1/2 c. sugar
1 egg, beaten
1/2 c. milk
1-1/4 t. vanilla extract

2 T. butter
1 qt. fresh strawberries, hulled
   and sliced
Garnish: whipped topping and
   strawberry slices

Sift flour, baking powder and sugar together; blend in egg, milk and vanilla. Pour into a greased and floured 9" round baking pan; bake at 350 degrees for 15 to 20 minutes. Turn cake out onto a wire rack, split in half horizontally while warm and spread bottom layer with butter and as many strawberries as desired. Replace top layer; top with whipped topping and garnish with strawberry halves. Serves 8.

Top shortcake with a strawberry fan...starting at the tip, cut a strawberry into thin slices almost to the stem. Carefully spread slices to form a fan.

Cinnamon-Pear Crisp

Vicki Cappola
Clarksville, IN

Serve warm with ice cream.

7 pears, peeled, cored and sliced
1/2 c. butter, softened
1 c. sugar

1 c. all-purpose flour
cinnamon and sugar to taste

Place pears in a greased 13"x9" baking pan. In a separate bowl, combine butter, sugar and flour until crumbly. Spread mixture evenly over pears; sprinkle with cinnamon and sugar to taste. Bake at 350 degrees for 45 minutes or until golden and bubbly. Makes 12 servings.

An old-fashioned pitcher and bowl pair up nicely to keep beverages chilled. Fill the bowl with ice and the pitcher with lemonade, then just nestle the pitcher in the bowl!

Grandma's Date-Nut Bread

Sue Wrobel
LaCrosse, WI

This is my favorite recipe for two good reasons...it's simple to make and tastes great!

1/2 c. chopped dates
1 c. boiling water
1 t. baking soda
1 c. brown sugar, packed

1 egg
1-1/4 c. all-purpose flour
1 c. nuts, chopped
1 t. vanilla extract

In a small bowl, combine chopped dates, boiling water, and baking soda; set aside. Beat together brown sugar and egg for about 2 minutes in a separate mixing bowl. Combine both mixtures, flour, nuts and vanilla; pour into a 9"x5" greased and floured loaf pan. Bake about 45 minutes or until pick inserted in center comes out clean; let stand in pan for 5 minutes. Turn out on a wire rack to cool. Makes 8 servings.

Create a cookie bouquet...guests will love it! Fill a terra cotta pot with florists' foam that's cut to fit inside; cover the foam with moss. Place freshly baked and decorated cookies on wooden skewers and just tuck into the foam.

Potlucks & Carry-Ins

Saucy Ham & Potato Bake

Lisa Quick
Clarksburg, MD

*Filled with melted cheese and potatoes, this is one of those
casseroles everyone likes.*

2 T. onion, chopped
1/4 c. butter or margarine
1/4 c. all-purpose flour
1 t. salt
1/2 t. dry mustard
1/8 t. pepper

1-1/2 c. milk
2 c. shredded Cheddar cheese,
  divided
6 c. potatoes, sliced
1/2 lb. cooked ham, cubed

Sauté onion in butter or margarine; blend in flour, salt, mustard and
pepper. Gradually add milk, stirring constantly until thickened; mix in
1-1/2 cups cheese and stir until melted. Remove from heat; toss in
potatoes and coat. Pour into a greased 13"x9" baking dish; arrange
ham and remaining cheese on top. Bake at 350 degrees for
30 minutes. Serves 6.

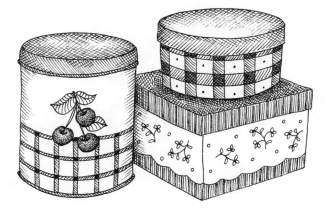

*Cooked beans add extra flavor to hearty soups and stews. Just
mash and freeze in an ice cube tray. Store them in freezer
bags, then just toss in the stockpot when needed.*

Chicken-Mushroom Casserole

Tammy Brown
Boaz, AL

So yummy...this dish won't last long.

2 lbs. boneless, skinless chicken breasts, boiled
10-3/4 oz. can cream of mushroom soup
10-3/4 oz. can cream of chicken soup
8-oz. carton sour cream
1/2 c. butter, melted
1/2 to 1 c. potato chips, crushed

Shred chicken and place in bottom of 13"x9" greased baking dish; set aside. Heat soups and sour cream in a medium saucepan until boiling; remove from heat and pour over chicken. Toss butter with potato chips; sprinkle over chicken mixture. Bake at 350 degrees for 30 minutes until browned and bubbly. Makes 8 servings.

Cream Soup Base

Peggy Salaets
Nampa, ID

Save pantry space...one batch of mix equals 7 cans of soup!

2 c. powdered milk
3/4 c. cornstarch
1/4 c. chicken bouillon granules
2 t. dried onion flakes
2 t. pepper
2 t. dried basil
2 t. dried thyme

Shake all ingredients together in an airtight container. Stir 1/2 cup soup base in 2 cups water to equal one can of cream soup. Recipe equals 7 cans of creamed soup.

Homestyle Baked Spaghetti

Marlene Lambie
Overland Park, KS

*A great casserole to share with family & friends...this
makes enough to feed our many grandchildren.*

8-oz. pkg. cream cheese,
  softened
1-1/2 c. sour cream
2 to 3 T. onion, grated
12-oz. pkg. fine egg noodles,
  cooked
2 lbs. ground beef, browned

2 t. salt
3 6-oz. cans tomato paste
2 c. water
2 t. sugar
1 t. pepper
Garnish: Parmesan cheese,
  grated

Blend cream cheese, sour cream and onion; stir in cooked noodles.
Place in bottom of 3-quart casserole dish; set aside. Combine meat,
salt, tomato paste, water, sugar and pepper in a saucepan; heat
thoroughly. Pour over noodles; sprinkle with Parmesan cheese. Bake
at 350 degrees for 45 minutes. Serves 8.

*No more flimsy paper plates at the next potluck...they'll fit
nice and snug inside a Frisbee® and, after lunch, it makes
a terrific gift for everyone to take home!*

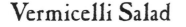
Vermicelli Salad

Vickie

Perfect for a potluck...this salad is made the night before.

16-oz. pkg. vermicelli, cooked
   and drained
4 T. olive oil
2 t. lemon juice
1/4 c. sliced olives
1 onion, chopped

1 green pepper, chopped
2 c. mayonnaise
6 cherry tomatoes, sliced
salt, pepper and garlic salt to
   taste

Marinate cooled noodles in oil and lemon juice for at least 6 hours.
Combine remaining ingredients; toss with noodles and chill salad for
several more hours before serving. Serves 8.

*Lay squares of pizza dough over inverted oiled custard cups,
then bake at 350 degrees until golden. Gently remove, turn
right side-up and let cool. . .individual
bread bowls for serving salad!*

Grannie's Meat Loaf

Mary Fry
Summerville, SC

Delicious warm or cold for sandwiches...the secret's in the sauce.

1 lb. ground beef
1 onion, grated
1 egg

2 slices bread, cubed
1 T. catsup
1 T. tomato sauce

Combine all ingredients in a medium mixing bowl; place into a 9"x5" loaf pan. Bake at 350 degrees for 45 minutes; drain excess fat. Pour sauce over the top; return to oven to bake 45 more minutes or until done. Makes 8 servings.

Sauce:

8-oz. can tomato sauce
2 T. catsup
1 t. dry mustard

1 t. vinegar
2 t. Worcestershire sauce
1 T. sugar

Mix all ingredients together until well blended.

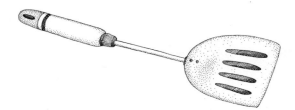

Kitchen utensils make a whimsical valance for a kitchen window. Secure a tension rod across the top of the window and suspend utensils on the rod with s-hooks...so clever!

Angel Rolls

*Kim Schooler
Norman, OK*

At our home, it's just not Sunday dinner without angel rolls.

1 pkg. active dry yeast	1/2 c. sugar
1/4 c. warm water	1 t. salt
1 c. milk, scalded	1/2 c. oil
2 eggs	4 c. all-purpose flour

Mix yeast with warm water; set aside. In another bowl, beat milk, eggs, sugar and salt together. Combine yeast mixture with oil; stir into milk mixture. Add flour; cover and let rest overnight. Turn dough onto a lightly floured surface; divide into 2 pieces and roll out each to 1/4-inch thickness. Do not work flour into dough. Cut each portion into 8 pie-shaped wedges; roll up, crescent roll-style, and place on greased baking sheet. Let rise until double in bulk; bake at 375 degrees for 12 minutes. Makes 16 servings.

*My mother's menu consisted of two choices: take it or leave it.
-Buddy Hackett*

Three-Bean Salad

Carol Eberly
Harrisonburg, VA

Handed down from my grandmother to me, this is my favorite salad.

16-oz. can green beans, drained
16-oz. can yellow beans, drained
16-oz. can kidney beans, rinsed and drained
1 onion, sliced

3/4 c. sugar
2/3 c. vinegar
1/3 c. oil
1 t. salt
1/4 t. pepper
1/4 t. dried oregano

Mix beans and onion together in a serving bowl; set aside. Combine remaining ingredients in a saucepan and heat until sugar dissolves; pour over bean mixture. Refrigerate at least 12 hours prior to serving. Makes 12 servings.

So much nicer than metal or plastic..an old-fashioned painted barrel can become a clever trash bin for your next get-together. Remember to tuck in a plastic liner to protect it.

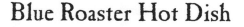

Blue Roaster Hot Dish

Cynthia McMullin
La Crosse, WI

I remember Mom making this whenever she needed a dish for a special gathering. I added rutabagas to her original recipe the year my brother planted too many in the garden!

2 lbs. ground beef, browned
2 c. rutabagas, chopped
5 lbs. potatoes, chopped
1 onion, chopped

1 lb. carrots, sliced
32-oz. can tomato sauce
16-oz. can stewed tomatoes
salt and pepper to taste

Mix all ingredients together and place in large roaster; bake 1-1/2 hours at 350 degrees. Makes 8 to 10 servings.

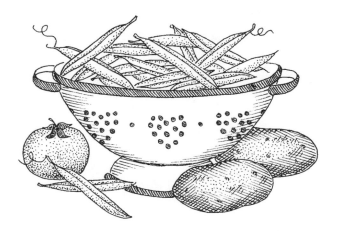

Having a neighborhood gathering to welcome a new family? Be sure to give them a local map so finding the grocery store, pharmacy, vet and post office is easy. Have all the neighbors jot down their favorite fun places to visit, too.

Quick & Easy Chili

JoAnn Drescher
Utica, NY

While the chili's simmering make some cornbread...together,
they're a perfect combination!

1 lb. ground beef
1 T. oil
1 onion, chopped
2 cloves garlic, chopped
2 15-1/2 oz. cans kidney beans,
    undrained

10-3/4 oz. can tomato soup
1/2 c. water
1 T. vinegar
2 T. chili powder
1/8 t. salt
1/8 t. pepper

Brown ground beef in oil. Add onion and garlic; sauté until tender. Mix in beans, tomato soup, water, vinegar, chili powder, salt and pepper; stir well. After mixture begins to boil, reduce heat and let simmer for 30 minutes. Makes 6 servings.

Chili Powder

Lori Burris
Gooseberry Patch

So easy to make your own...add more cayenne if you like it hot.

3/4 c. crushed red pepper flakes
1/4 c. cumin
2-1/2 T. garlic powder

1 T. oregano
1 T. cayenne pepper

Place all ingredients in a blender; purée until powdered. Let powder settle before removing lid; pour into a storage container. Makes about one cup.

A perfect summer day is when the sun is shining, the breeze
is blowing, the birds are singing and the
lawn mower is broken.
-James Dent

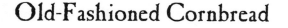

Old-Fashioned Cornbread

Terry Williams
Irvine, PA

Our family loves this buttered and warm from the oven or cold and topped with berries.

3/4 c. yellow cornmeal
1 c. all-purpose flour
2/3 c. sugar
3/4 t. salt

3-1/2 t. baking powder
1 c. milk
1 egg, beaten
1/4 c. oil

Stir together dry ingredients; make a well in the mix. Blend milk, egg and oil together; pour into the well of dry ingredients. Beat thoroughly. Pour into greased 8"x8" square pan; bake at 400 degrees for 22 to 25 minutes. Center will be set and edges golden brown when done. Makes 16 servings.

If you need extra chairs for a get-together, search flea markets ahead of time for old metal lawn chairs like Grandma had in her backyard. Just give them a face lift with a new coat of paint.

Dilled Chicken

Cathy Harmon
Red Lion, PA

A fast & easy, one-pan meal.

1/3 c. all-purpose flour
1 t. salt
1/2 t. paprika
4 skinless, boneless chicken
    breasts, halved
2 T. oil

2 c. chicken broth
1/4 c. fresh dill, chopped
8 new potatoes
3/4 lb. green beans, trimmed
salt and pepper to taste

Mix flour, salt and paprika together; coat chicken and set aside remaining flour mixture. Heat oil in a deep large skillet over medium heat; add chicken and cook 3 minutes. Turn chicken, cook an additional 3 minutes and remove from skillet. Stir reserved flour mixture into drippings; gradually stir in chicken broth, then dill. Return chicken to skillet and bring to a boil. Add potatoes, reduce heat, cover and simmer 10 minutes. Add green beans, cover and simmer 10 minutes more or until chicken and potatoes are tender. Sprinkle with salt, pepper and remaining dill. Simmer another 1-1/2 to 2 hours. Makes 4 servings.

Bring along colorful vintage salt & pepper shakers to the next carry-in...they'll add a little whimsy!

Oriental Spinach Salad

Tammy Munn
Tampa, FL

Ginger and soy sauce give this salad a great tangy taste.

2 T. white vinegar
2 T. soy sauce
1-1/2 t. sugar
1/2 t. ground ginger
2 green onions, minced

3 T. oil
6 c. fresh spinach, torn
2 c. Chinese cabbage, shredded
2 t. toasted sesame seed

Blend vinegar, soy sauce, sugar and ginger together. Stir in onion and oil. Add spinach, cabbage and sesame seed; toss lightly. Serves 8.

Give salads a fresh new taste... instead of using white vinegar when making salad dressing, add a splash of fruit juice or fruit-flavored vinegar.

Extra Special Biscuits

Rhonda Millerman
Cameron, WI

You only need to taste them to see why they're "extra special."

2 c. all-purpose flour	4 t. baking powder
1/2 t. salt	1/3 c. shortening
1-1/2 t. sugar	2/3 c. milk

Mix flour, salt, sugar and baking powder together; cut in shortening. Add milk and stir until dough forms a ball. Turn onto a floured surface and gently knead 10 times. Roll dough to 1/2 inch thickness; cut with a biscuit cutter. Place on a greased baking sheet; bake at 350 degrees for 20 minutes. Makes 10 servings.

It works like a charm... lightly press a metal ice cube divider into rolled-out biscuit dough. When the biscuits are baked, they'll easily separate at the dividing lines.

Ham & Bean Soup

Mary Murray
Gooseberry Patch

*Add everything to the slow cooker the night
before...what could be easier?*

3 c. parsnips, chopped
2 c. carrots, chopped
1 c. onion, chopped
1-1/2 c. dry Great Northern
    beans
5 c. water

1-1/2 lbs. smoked ham hocks
2 cloves garlic, minced
2 t. salt
1/2 t. pepper
1/4 t. hot pepper sauce

Place parsnips, carrots and onion in a 5-quart slow cooker; top with
beans. Add water, ham, garlic, salt, pepper and hot pepper sauce.
Cover and cook on high for 6 to 7 hours or until beans are tender.
Remove meat and bones; set aside. When cool enough to handle, cut
meat into bite-size pieces and return to slow cooker; heat through.
Serves 6.

*Dessert in a
jiffy...mist clusters of
chilled grapes or
cherries with water
and roll in sugar.*

Best-Ever Macaroni & Cheese

Marion Stead
Dansville, NY

*No get-together is complete unless there's macaroni & cheese
and this version is just the best!*

8-oz. pkg. elbow macaroni,
    cooked and drained
16-oz. carton cottage cheese
3/4 c. sour cream
1 c. shredded sharp Cheddar
    cheese

1 egg, beaten
1 t. salt
1/8 t. pepper
2 t. onion, grated
Garnish: Italian bread crumbs,
    paprika and dried parsley

Combine all ingredients in a 2-quart casserole dish. Bake, uncovered,
at 350 degrees for 45 minutes. Garnish with bread crumbs, paprika
and parsley. Makes 6 servings.

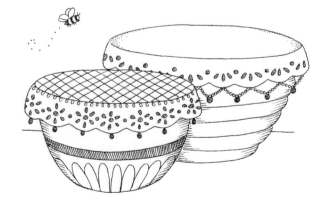

*Sew small buttons around the edges of colorful handkerchiefs
or pretty fabric squares, then lay over the top of a pitcher of
lemonade or bowls of tasty side dishes...keeps
buzzing bees away!*

Honey-Butter Rolls

Zoe Bennett
Columbia, SC

Golden and light, these never last long!

1-1/2 c. whole-wheat flour
3-1/4 c. all-purpose flour,
   divided
2 pkgs. active dry yeast
2 t. salt

1/2 t. baking soda
1-1/2 c. plain yogurt
12 c. water
3 T. butter
2 T. honey

Combine whole-wheat flour, 1/2 cup all-purpose flour, yeast, salt and baking soda in a mixing bowl. In a saucepan over low heat, heat yogurt, water, butter and honey to 120 to 130 degrees on a candy thermometer; pour over dry ingredients, blending well. Beat on medium speed for 3 minutes. Add enough remaining flour to form a soft dough. Turn onto a floured surface; knead until smooth and elastic, about 6 to 8 minutes. Place into a greased bowl, turning once to grease top. Cover and let rise in a warm place until double in bulk. Punch down dough; divide into 24 pieces. Roll each piece into a 9-inch rope. To form S-shaped rolls, coil each end of rope toward center in opposite directions. Place 3 inches apart on greased baking sheets. Cover and let rise until double in bulk. Bake at 400 degrees for 15 minutes or until golden brown. Brush tops with melted butter, if desired. Makes 2 dozen.

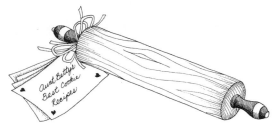

A special gift to a new bride...pass down Grandma's rolling pin, along with some of her favorite recipes.

Creamy Pecan Chicken

Kathy Grashoff
Fort Wayne, IN

Sprinkle some extra pecans on top for added crunch.

8 boneless, skinless chicken
   breasts
1/2 t. salt
1/8 t. pepper
1/2 c. butter, melted

1/4 c. plus 2 T. Dijon mustard,
   divided
1 c. chopped pecans
16-oz. carton sour cream
1/3 c. water

Sprinkle chicken with salt and pepper then place in a greased 13"x9" baking dish. Stir together butter and 1/4 cup mustard; pour over chicken breasts. Sprinkle pecans over the top; bake, uncovered, at 375 degrees for 35 minutes or until juices run clear when chicken is pierced. Remove chicken to a serving platter; reserve drippings. In a large saucepan, combine remaining mustard, drippings, sour cream and water. Cook over medium heat until bubbly; stirring constantly. To serve, pour mix over chicken. Makes 8 servings.

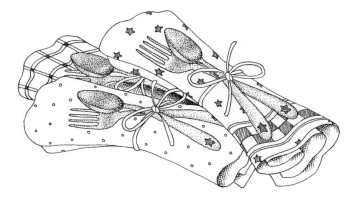

Wrap silverware in colorful vintage-looking dishtowels...very pretty and much sturdier than paper napkins.

Golden Cheddar Biscuits

Julie Wise
Delaware, OH

Melt-in-your-mouth delicious!

1/4 c. shortening
1 t. sugar
1 c. all-purpose flour
2 t. baking powder
1/4 t. salt

1 t. garlic powder
1 egg
1/3 c. milk
1 c. grated Cheddar cheese

Cream shortening and sugar. Mix dry ingredients together; add to shortening and sugar mixture. Blend in egg, milk and cheese. Divide mixture equally into a greased muffin pan and bake at 400 degrees for 20 minutes or until golden brown. Makes one dozen.

Herbed Butter

Yvonne Hanlon
San Bruno, CA

Great on warm rolls or grilled vegetables.

4 cloves garlic
1 lb. butter
1 c. fresh parsley
1/4 c. fresh thyme

1/4 c. fresh oregano
1/8. c. fresh winter savory
1/4 c. fresh rosemary
1/4 c. fresh chives

Purée all ingredients in food processor. Pack in a crock and keep refrigerated. Makes one pound.

Mom's Sunday Potatoes

Stephanie Gerig
Woodburn, OH

Mashed potatoes just don't get any better than this.

8 to 10 potatoes, peeled, cubed,
    boiled and drained
8-oz. pkg. sour cream
8-oz. pkg. cream cheese,
    softened

1 t. garlic salt
3 T. butter
1/2 t. paprika

Mash potatoes in a large mixing bowl with an electric mixer; add sour cream, cream cheese and garlic salt. Mix well; pour into a 2-quart casserole dish. Dot with butter; sprinkle with paprika. Bake at 350 degrees for 30 minutes. Makes 12 servings.

Tangy Onion Gravy

Donna Zink
Lapeer, MI

Served over mashed potatoes, pork chops or slices of roast beef,
this is the best gravy imaginable!

2 cubes beef bouillon
3 c. water, divided
4 T. all-purpose flour

1-1/2 oz. pkg. dry onion soup
    mix

Dissolve bouillon in 1-1/2 cups water; set aside. Add flour to a medium saucepan; gradually add bouillon mixture, stirring until smooth. Mix in onion soup mix and remaining water; bring to a boil. Cover; boil 5 to 8 minutes. Makes about 2-1/2 cups.

Pork Chop & Rice Casserole

Karla Harrington
Anchorage, AK

Pork chops and apples always seem to be paired together...there's just something wonderful about them!

8 pork chops
salt and pepper to taste
1 T. oil
1/2 c. onion, chopped
2 T. butter
2-2/3 c. rice, cooked

1 c. apples, diced
1 c. dried prunes, chopped
1-1/2 t. salt
1/8 t. pepper
1/8 t. poultry seasoning

Salt and pepper pork chops, then brown in oil in a large oven-safe skillet; drain and set aside. In same pan, sauté onion in butter until soft. Add remaining ingredients except for meat, mixing well. Arrange pork chops on rice mixture; cover and bake at 350 degrees about 45 minutes or until done. Serves 8.

Sometimes it takes an entire day to write a recipe...it's really like writing a little short story.
-Julia Child

Garden Vegetable Lasagna

Wendy Lee Paffenroth
Pine Island, NY

Toss in any of your favorite veggies to make this terrific dish.

10-oz. pkg. frozen chopped
    spinach, thawed and drained
1 c. carrots, thinly sliced
1 c. zucchini, thinly sliced
3 c. ricotta cheese, divided
1 egg, beaten
16-oz. pkg. lasagna noodles,
    cooked and drained

1 onion, chopped
2 T. oil
2 T. all-purpose flour
1/8 t. pepper
1 c. chicken broth
1/2 c. grated Parmesan cheese
2 tomatoes, sliced
1 c. shredded mozzarella cheese

In a large bowl, mix spinach, carrots, zucchini, 1/2 cup ricotta cheese and egg; set aside. Place one layer of the noodles into a 13"x9" baking pan; spread 1/2 of the vegetable mixture over the top. Repeat the layers ending with noodles. Sauté onion in oil until tender; stir in flour, pepper, broth and 1/2 cup ricotta. Cook and stir until it starts to come to a boil; remove from heat. Pour flour mixture over the lasagna noodles; sprinkle with Parmesan cheese. Cover with aluminum foil; bake at 350 degrees for 45 minutes. Uncover; put under broiler for a few minutes until top starts to brown. Remove from broiler and top with tomatoes and mozzarella. Return to broiler just until cheese begins to melt. Makes 12 servings.

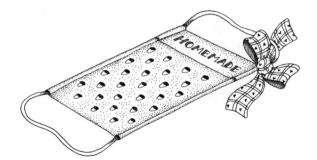

There is nothing better than the ecouragement
of a good friend.
-Katherine Hathaway

Dilly Bread

Irene Senne
Aplington, IA

*Great for sandwiches or spread with cream cheese
and sprinkled with chives.*

1 pkg. active dry yeast
1/4 c. warm water
1 c. cottage cheese
2 T. sugar
1 T. onion, minced
4 T. butter, divided
2-1/2 t. dill weed

1 t. salt
1/4 t. baking soda
1 egg
2-1/4 to 2-1/2 c. all-purpose
    flour
2 T. butter, melted
1 T. coarse salt

Sprinkle yeast over warm water; set aside. Heat cottage cheese until just warm; add to a mixing bowl. Stir in sugar, onion, 2 tablespoons butter, dill weed, salt, soda, egg and yeast mixture; add flour to form a stiff dough. Knead several times on a lightly floured surface; cover and let dough double in bulk. Punch down; divide into 2 loaves. Place each in a greased, one-pound coffee can; let rise until double in bulk again. Brush tops with butter and sprinkle with coarse salt; bake at 350 degrees for 30 to 35 minutes. Serves 16.

*Painted clothespins
make clever
placecard holders.
Write each guest's
name on a square
of card stock and
slip inside the
clothespin.*

Hamburger Stroganoff

Kathie Williams
Oakland City, IN

Easy to make and tasty...that makes this one of our favorites.

1 lb. ground beef
3 slices bacon
1/2 c. onion, chopped
1/4 t. paprika
3/4 t. salt
1/8 t. pepper

10 3/4-oz. can cream of mushroom soup
1 c. sour cream
12-oz. pkg. egg noodles, cooked
 and drained
2 T. butter

Brown beef with bacon; add onion and cook until soft. Drain and add
paprika, salt and pepper; mix well. Stir in soup; cook, uncovered, over
low heat for 20 minutes, stirring often. Add sour cream and heat
through without boiling. Toss noodles with butter; top with stroganoff.
Makes 6 to 8 servings.

Mom's Noodles

Cheryl Kimball
Plymouth, MI

*Whether they're for chicken & noodles or tuna noodle casserole,
nothing tastes as good as homemade.*

2 c. all-purpose flour
1/2 t. salt

2 eggs

Sift flour and salt together. Gradually mix in eggs until a stiff dough
forms. Knead a few minutes on a lightly floured surface. Roll out to
1/4-inch thickness. Let stand for one hour or more. Cut into long
strips, 1/8-inch wide for fine noodles or 1/2-inch wide for broad
noodles; separate and let air dry thoroughly. When ready to cook,
place noodles in 3 to 4 quarts boiling water for 20 minutes or until
tender; drain. Makes one pound.

City Chicken

Elizabeth Andrus
Gooseberry Patch

During the 1940's, meals were often called by a name other than the actual ingredients. Imagination was needed when items were hard to come by.

2 lbs. boneless pork, cubed
1/2 c. all-purpose flour
1/2 t. garlic salt
1/4 t. pepper
1/2 c. margarine
14-1/2 oz. can chicken broth

1-1/2 oz. pkg. dry onion soup
   mix
1 c. water
1/2 c. milk
1 T. cornstarch

Thread pork closely together on 6 wooden skewers; set aside. Combine flour, garlic salt and pepper; coat pork. Melt margarine in a large skillet over medium heat; brown pork skewers on all sides until golden in color, about 15 minutes. Mix chicken broth, onion soup and water together in a mixing bowl; pour over pork in skillet. Cover and simmer on low heat for 1-1/2 hours; remove pork skewers and set aside. Add milk and cornstarch to broth mixture; stir until thick and bubbly. Pour over pork skewers before serving. Makes 6 servings.

Try using dry bread crumbs instead of adding flour for thick and creamy casseroles.

Swedish Ham Balls

Pat Fender
Memphis, MO

Keep warm in a slow cooker, then just watch them disappear!

1-1/2 lb. cooked ham, ground
1 lb. ground pork
2 c. bread crumbs
2 eggs, slightly beaten
1 c. milk

1-1/2 c. brown sugar, packed
1/2 c. vinegar
1/2 c. water
1 t. dry mustard

Mix ham, pork, bread crumbs, eggs and milk together; shape into walnut-size balls and place in a 13"x9" ungreased baking dish. Blend brown sugar, vinegar, water and mustard together in a separate mixing bowl; pour over ham balls. Bake at 275 degrees for 2 hours, turning balls over after one hour. Makes about 3 dozen.

Tuck popsicles in a large ice-filled bucket or colorful bowl...a fun way to serve a summertime treat!

Cheddar-Broccoli Soup

Linda Seamans
Pulaski, NY

*My children and grandchildren love it when I make this
cheesy soup. Try it...you're in for a treat!*

1 onion, diced
4 T. butter
4 T. cornstarch
1/2 t. pepper

4 c. milk
1 c. sharp Cheddar cheese, cubed
1 c. cooked ham, cubed
1 bunch broccoli, chopped

Sauté onion in butter until tender; add cornstarch and pepper, mixing
well. Slowly pour in milk, stirring constantly. Add cheese; stir until
melted. Mix in ham and broccoli; cook on low heat for one hour.
Serves 8.

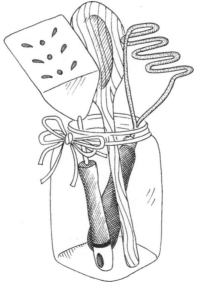

*To make sure casseroles arrive at get-togethers warm and
bubbly, wrap the baking dish in aluminum foil, then
surround it with several layers of newspaper.*

Italian Cream Cake

Kim Schooler
Norman, OK

A tried & true recipe handed down from Grandma.

2 c. sugar
1/2 c. butter
1/2 c. shortening
1/2 c. buttermilk
2 c. all-purpose flour
1 t. baking soda

1/2 t. salt
5 eggs, separated
1 c. chopped pecans
2 c. flaked coconut
Garnish: flaked coconut and
    chopped pecans

Combine sugar, butter, shortening and buttermilk in a large mixing bowl; set aside. Mix flour, baking soda and salt in a separate mixing bowl; set aside. Alternately, add the flour mixture and the egg yolks to the sugar mix, blending well. Stir in pecans and coconut; set aside. In a small bowl, beat egg whites until stiff. Fold into batter and pour into 2, 8" round greased and floured baking pans. Bake at 350 degrees for 20 to 30 minutes. Turn out on a rack to cool. Frost and sprinkle with coconut and pecans, if desired. Makes 8 servings.

Frosting:

8-oz. pkg. cream cheese,
    softened
1/2 c. butter

1 t. vanilla extract
1 lb. powdered sugar
3/4 t. butter flavoring

Cream all ingredients together.

Yum... bite-size, chocolate-covered bananas! Just slice bananas and dip in melted chocolate. Freeze on a baking sheet then place in plastic zipping bags. Toss bags in an ice-filled cooler and tote to the potluck... the kids will love 'em!

The Easiest Peanut Butter Cookie

Jodi Metcalf
Camby, IN

Don't let the simplicity of this recipe fool you, these cookies are awesome!

2 eggs
2 c. sugar

2 c. peanut butter

Blend together eggs and sugar until smooth; add peanut butter, mixing well. Roll into walnut-size balls; place onto ungreased baking sheets. With a fork, press a criss-cross pattern on top of each ball to flatten slightly; bake at 375 degrees for 7 to 9 minutes. Makes about 2 dozen.

Lemon Pie

Donna Cole
Atkins, AR

My grandmother's never-fail recipe.

8-oz. can sweetened condensed milk
8-oz. pkg. cream cheese, softened

1/3 c. lemon juice
9-inch graham cracker pie crust, unbaked

Blend milk and cream cheese together until smooth; add lemon juice and blend until thickened. Pour into crust; refrigerate at least one hour. Serves 8.

No-Bake Strawberry Cheesecake

Vickie

This easy version is ready to enjoy in no time at all!

4 oz. cream cheese, softened
1/4 c. sugar
1/2 c. sour cream
1 t. vanilla extract
4 oz. whipped topping

1 c. strawberry glaze
9-inch graham cracker pie crust,
    unbaked
1 pt. strawberries, thinly sliced

Beat cream cheese until smooth; gradually beat in sugar. Blend in sour cream and vanilla. Fold in whipped topping; blending well. Spread a thin layer of glaze over the bottom of the crust; layer strawberry slices on glaze. Cover with an additional layer of glaze; smooth cream cheese mixture on the top. Cover and chill until set. Makes 8 servings.

Bite-size cheesecakes always disappear fast at potlucks! Any favorite recipe can be used...just bake in mini muffin pans.

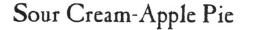

Sour Cream-Apple Pie

Lois Vardaro
East Northport, NY

I've been making this pie for 20 years...try it, it's delicious!

9-inch pie crust, unbaked
2 c. Rome apples, cored, peeled
   and chopped
1/3 c. plus 2 T. all-purpose flour,
   divided
1/2 c. plus 1/3 c. sugar, divided

1/4 t. salt
1 c. sour cream
1 egg, beaten
1-1/2 t. vanilla extract
1/2 t. cinnamon
1/4 c. butter

Place pie crust in pie pan; add apples. Combine 2 tablespoons flour,
1/2 cup sugar and salt in a separate bowl; add sour cream, egg and
vanilla. Beat until smooth; pour over apples. Bake at 425 degrees for
15 minutes; reduce heat to 350 degrees and bake for an
additional 30 minutes. Combine cinnamon, butter, remaining flour and
sugar; sprinkle on top of pie. Bake at 400 degrees an additional
10 minutes. Makes 8 servings.

*Happiness is a butterfly, which, when pursued, is always just
beyond your grasp, but which, if you will sit down
quietly, may alight upon you.*
-Nathaniel Hawthorne

Vermont Maple Cookies

Pam Wagner
Ford City, PA

It's the maple-butter glaze that makes these cookies so good.

1/2 c. shortening
1/2 c. sugar
1 c. brown sugar, packed
2 eggs
1 c. sour cream

1 T. maple flavoring
2-3/4 c. all-purpose flour
1/2 t. baking soda
1 t. salt
1 c. chopped nuts

Combine shortening, sugars and eggs thoroughly; stir in sour cream and maple flavoring. In a separate bowl, mix flour, baking soda and salt together; blend into sugar mixture. Stir in nuts and drop by rounded tablespoonfuls, about 2 inches apart on a greased baking sheet. Bake at 375 degrees for about 10 minutes or until almost no imprint shows when lightly touched. Cool; ice with glaze. Makes about 4 dozen.

Maple-Butter Glaze:

1/2 c. butter
2 c. powdered sugar

2 t. maple flavoring
3 T. hot water

Heat butter until golden brown; mix in powdered sugar and flavoring. Stir in water gradually until icing is smooth.

Give some fresh color to traditional folding chairs. . . cover each with a slip cover made from cheery gingham!

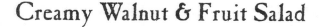
Creamy Walnut & Fruit Salad

Carol Suehiro
Renton, WA

This salad has become a family favorite...get-togethers just wouldn't be the same without it.

3-oz. pkg. lemon gelatin
1 c. hot water
1/2 c. cottage cheese
1 c. whipping cream, whipped
1/2 c. chopped walnuts

1/2 c. maraschino cherries,
   quartered
1 c. crushed pineapple, drained
Garnish: maraschino cherries,
   halved

Dissolve gelatin in hot water and chill until partially set. Fold in cottage cheese, whipping cream, walnuts, maraschino cherries and crushed pineapple. Pour into a one-quart serving dish; chill until firm. Decorate with a half cherry on top of each square. Makes 16 servings.

Always serve too much hot fudge sauce on hot fudge sundaes.
It makes people overjoyed and puts them in your debt.
-Judith Olney

Country Pasta Dish

Candi Sparrow
Davie, FL

Tuck this tasty salad in an old-fashioned pickle jar,
easy to tote and won't spill!

3 c. sliced mushrooms
1 onion, chopped
3 cloves garlic, minced
3 T. olive oil
4 T. margarine

6 plum tomatoes, chopped
1 c. grated Romano cheese
12-oz. pkg. egg noodles, cooked
   and drained

Sauté mushrooms, onion and garlic in oil and margarine until tender; stir in tomatoes. Add Romano cheese; simmer 15 minutes. Pour over noodles; toss before serving. Serves 4.

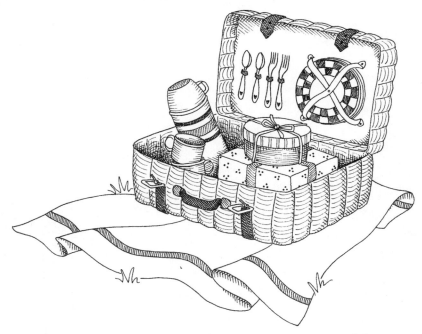

Divided baskets are just right for silverware caddies...tie a cheery bow around the handle and it's ready for any potluck!

Caesar-Style Salad Dressing

Amy Jonsson
Half Moon Bay, CA

Pour over a garden fresh salad of romaine lettuce and top with your choice of croutons for an easy potluck dish.

1 T. mayonnaise
1/2 c. Parmesan cheese, grated
1/4 c. lemon juice
2 cloves garlic, minced
1 t. Worcestershire sauce

1/2 t. salt
1/2 t. pepper
1.58-oz. tube anchovy paste
1/2 c. oil

Combine all ingredients except paste and oil in a blender; blend well. Gradually add 1/4 tube anchovy paste and oil with blender on low speed; continue blending until thick and creamy. Cover and refrigerate up to 5 days; let stand at room temperature for 15 minutes before serving. Makes about 1-1/4 cups.

A messy kitchen is a happy kitchen
and this kitchen is delirious!
-Unknown

Scalloped Potatoes

Beth Kelly
Glassport, PA

Buttery, cheesy potatoes with thick slices of kielbasa...yum!

10 potatoes, peeled, cubed,
    boiled and drained
1 c. butter, melted
1-1/3 c. all-purpose flour
6 c. milk
salt and pepper to taste
1 t. dried parsley

1 t. onion salt
1 onion, chopped
2 c. shredded Cheddar cheese,
    divided
1/2 lb. kielbasa, chopped

Melt butter in a saucepan; whisk in flour until smooth. Add milk; stir until smooth and thickened. Add salt, pepper, parsley flakes and onion salt; set aside. Pour a thin layer of sauce into a 2-quart greased casserole dish; layer half the onion, cheese, kielbasa then potatoes. Pour 1/4 cup remaining sauce over mixture; then repeat layers, reserving 1/4 cup cheese. Top with any remaining sauce and cheese. Bake one hour at 350 degrees. Serves 10 to 15.

What I say is that, if a man really likes potatoes,
he must be a pretty decent sort of fellow.
-A. A. Milne

Stewed Tomato Dumplings

Eula Preston
Zanesville, OH

True comfort food...warm and filling.

2 14-1/2 oz. cans of stewed   1/2 c. whipping cream
   tomatoes   sugar to taste
2 c. water

In a medium saucepan, combine ingredients; bring to a boil slowly, do not scald. Drop dumplings by teaspoonfuls into boiling mixture; boil, covered, for 12 to 15 minutes. Spoon into bowls; sprinkle with sugar, if desired. Makes 4 servings.

Dumplings:

1 c. all-purpose flour   1 T. shortening
1-1/2 t. baking powder   1/2 c. milk
1/2 t. salt

Sift flour, baking powder and salt together; cut in shortening until mixture resembles coarse crumbs. Gradually add milk, mixing lightly to form a soft dough.

Apricot Sherbet

LaVerne Fang
Joliet, IL

Substitute nectarines or peaches for a refreshing treat.

2 qts. apricots, peeled and pitted   1 t. lemon juice
1-1/2 c. sugar

Place apricots, a few at a time, in a blender; blend until smooth and creamy. Repeat with all apricots until blended mixture equals one quart; add sugar and lemon juice. Blend well; freeze. Makes 4 servings.

Make your own colored sugar for cookies and cupcakes. Just add a drop or two of food coloring to 1/4 cup sugar, blend well and let dry on wax paper overnight.

Family Reunions & Picnics

Southern Fried Chicken

Jo Ann

Remember all the good things that go with this...biscuits, coleslaw, mashed potatoes & gravy.

1 c. all-purpose flour
2 t. seasoned salt
1 t. baking powder
1/2 t. onion powder
1/4 t. cinnamon
1/2 t. ground ginger

1/2 t. garlic powder
1/4 t. pepper
2-1/2 to 3 lbs. chicken
1 egg, beaten
oil for deep frying

Place dry ingredients in large plastic bag and shake to blend. Dip chicken pieces in egg, then add to bag; toss to coat. Add enough oil to a large skillet to equal one inch; heat until a drop of water sizzles when dropped into oil. Fry chicken pieces, covered, 30 minutes or until tender and juices run clear, turning chicken every 8 minutes; drain on paper towels. Serves 4.

Add a little lemon-lime soda to fruit juice for a fizzy treat!

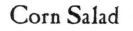

Corn Salad

Diane Long
Delaware, OH

A tasty change of pace from tossed salads.

2 c. canned corn
3/4 c. celery, sliced
1/4 c. green pepper, sliced

1/4 c. red pepper, sliced
1-1/2 T. onion, minced

Mix ingredients together and set aside. Prepare dressing and pour over corn mixture. Refrigerate for one hour before serving. Makes 6 servings.

Dressing:

1 c. oil
1/4 t. pepper
1 t. paprika

1 t. sugar
1/3 c. vinegar
salt to taste

Stir all ingredients together and shake to combine.

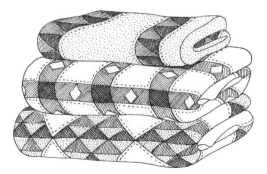

The family is one of nature's masterpieces.
-George Santayana

Sweet Cranberry Salad

Anna McMaster
Portland, OR

My grandmother's original recipe has been handed down
and enjoyed by three generations.

2 c. cranberries
2 c. sugar
2 3-oz. pkgs. lemon gelatin

4 c. warm water
1 c. celery, diced
1 c. chopped walnuts

Place cranberries in a food processor and pulse until finely chopped; stir in sugar and set aside. Dissolve lemon gelatin in water; chill until partly set. Add all other ingredients; chill until completely set. Serves 6.

Butternut Squash & Apples

Janice McCatty
Royal Oak, MI

Covered with a sweet sugared glaze.

2-lb. butternut squash, peeled
2 Rome apples, cored
1/4 c. brown sugar, packed

1 T. all-purpose flour
1 T. margarine, melted
1/4 t. salt

Cut squash in half lengthwise and discard seeds; cut each half into 1/2-inch thick slices and place in a greased 13"x9" baking dish. Slice apples into 8 wedges and layer over squash. Combine brown sugar, flour, margarine and salt in a small bowl; sprinkle over apples. Cover and bake at 350 degrees for 30 minutes; uncover and bake an additional 20 minutes or until squash is tender. Makes 6 servings.

Turn an old wheelbarrow into a grill! Insulate it with
6 inches of gravel or sand and cover with heavy aluminum
foil. Top with charcoal. . . a grill that goes anywhere!

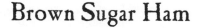

Brown Sugar Ham
Vickie

Not only tasty served warm, but sliced cold for sandwiches, too.

5-lb. fully-cooked ham
1-1/2 c. brown sugar, packed
3/4 c. soft bread crumbs
2 t. dry mustard

1/2 t. cinnamon
1/4 t. ground cloves
1/3 c. pineapple juice

Place ham in a large roaster and bake at 325 degrees for one hour. Remove from oven and score top of ham. Combine sugar, bread crumbs and spices; add juice and mix to form a thick paste. Spread over the ham. Increase oven to 350 degrees; bake 1/2 hour or until meat thermometer reaches 160 degrees. Baste with pan juices before slicing. Serves 10.

Pineapple-Peach Ham Glaze
Delinda Blakney
Bridgeview, IL

Not like traditional glazes, but simply delicious!

3/4 c. cola soda
12-oz. jar peach preserves
4 T. mustard

1-1/2 c. brown sugar, packed
15-3/4 oz. can pineapple chunks
12-oz. pkg. raisins

Combine all ingredients; baste ham every 30 minutes.

Blueberry Lemonade

Kathy Grashoff
Fort Wayne, IN

Family reunions mean the kids will be playing lots of games…keep them cool with tall, icy glasses of lemonade.

1/3 c. freshly squeezed lemon
   juice
2 c. water

2 c. blueberries
1/2 c. sugar
Garnish: lemon slices

Blend together lemon juice, water, blueberries and sugar until smooth in a blender. Pour through a wire-mesh strainer into a pitcher; discard fruit solids. Serve over ice; garnish with lemon slice. Makes about 4-1/2 cups.

Homemade Peach Lemonade

Cindy Kingren
Peoria, AZ

When you're looking for something really refreshing try this!

2 peaches, peeled, pitted and
   chopped
1 c. sugar

4 c. water
3/4 c. freshly squeezed lemon
   juice

Combine peaches, sugar and water in a saucepan; bring to a boil. Simmer until the sugar is dissolved, about 10 minutes. Allow to cool and strain through a sieve, pressing to extract as much juice as possible. Stir in lemon juice; serve in tall glasses over ice. Makes 4 servings.

Cherry Cola Salad

Marian Bates
Stephen, MN

I have shared this recipe with so many people. They love it because not only does it taste great, it's easy to make, too.

21-oz. can cherry pie filling
1-1/2 c. water
1/2 c. sugar

2 3-oz. pkgs. cherry gelatin
12-oz. can cola soda
Garnish: slivered almonds

Mix cherry pie filling, water, and sugar together; bring to a boil. While boiling, add gelatin. Remove from heat and stir until dissolved. Pour into a bowl and refrigerate until mixture is syrupy. Add cola slowly, as it will foam; chill until set. Make topping and spread evenly over the top; garnish with almonds. Makes 8 servings.

Topping:

16 marshmallows, melted
3-oz. pkg. cream cheese

1/2 pt. whipping cream, whipped

Combine melted marshmallows and cream cheese; mix well. Fold in whipped topping.

Happiness is not something you experience,
it's something you remember.
-Oscar Levant

Peanut Butter-Chocolate Bars

June Eier
Forest, OH

My kids and all their friends love these...you may have to make a double batch to keep them happy!

6 c. quick-cooking oats,
   uncooked
1 c. brown sugar, packed
3/4 c. corn syrup

2/3 c. shortening, melted
4-1/2 t. vanilla extract
1 c. chunky peanut butter
2 c. chocolate chips

Mix first six ingredients together; press into a 13"x9" baking pan. Bake at 375 degrees for 12 minutes. Remove from oven and immediately sprinkle with chocolate chips; spread when melted. Cool and cut into 24 bars.

Keep the little ones busy with an alphabet game while traveling to a picnic. Start with the letter "A" and say, "I'm going to a picnic and I'm going to bring ants." The next person must repeat the same phrase, remembering "A" is for ants, then add something of their own that begins with "B".

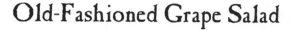
Old-Fashioned Grape Salad

Angie O'Keefe
Soddy Daisy, TN

This recipe, shared by a special friend, is terrific for potlucks...cool and creamy with crunchy pecans.

8 oz. sour cream
8-oz. pkg. cream cheese,
   softened
1/2 c. sugar

2-1/2 lbs. seedless grapes
1/2 c. brown sugar, packed
1/2 c. pecans, chopped

Combine sour cream, cream cheese and sugar; mix well. Stir in grapes to coat. Just before serving, sprinkle with brown sugar and pecans. Makes 10 to 12 servings.

Fill a galvanized bucket with ice and fresh fruit like cherries, grapes and apples. It's easy to carry and the fruit will stay chilled and delicious.

Crispy Oven-Fried Chicken

Brenda Doak
Gooseberry Patch

Unlike traditional fried chicken, this doesn't require careful watching. It's great hot or cold, in salads or on sandwiches!

2 eggs
4 T. butter, melted
1-1/4 c. corn flake cereal,
   crushed
1 T. dried parsley

1-1/2 t. poultry seasoning
1 t. dried basil
1/4 t. dried thyme
1/8 t. garlic powder
2-1/2 to 3 lbs. chicken

Beat eggs and butter together in a shallow bowl. In another bowl, toss together corn cereal and seasonings. Dip chicken pieces in egg mixture, then dredge in crumbs. Place in an ungreased shallow baking dish; bake at 375 degrees for 30 minutes. Gently turn; bake 25 to 30 minutes longer or until juices run clear when chicken is pierced. Serves 4 to 6.

Watermelon. . .you eat, you drink, you wash your face.
-Enrico Caruso

Mom's Potato Salad

Linda Scott-Hoag
Janesville, WI

This is the only potato salad I like!

4 to 5 new potatoes, boiled and
   chopped
1/3 c. onion, diced
salt and pepper to taste

2 hard-boiled eggs, chopped
1 T. mustard
1/4 c. mayonnaise

Combine all ingredients together in a large mixing bowl. Refrigerate
overnight to blend flavors. Serves 4.

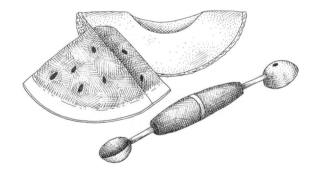

Homemade Mayonnaise

Kelly Alderson
Erie, PA

You'll be surprised at how easy this is to make...give it a try.

3 eggs, beaten
1/2 c. sugar
1/2 t. dry mustard

1 c. whipping cream
1/2 c. vinegar
1 t. salt

Combine eggs, sugar, mustard and cream in a double boiler over
medium heat; slowly add vinegar, mixing well. Heat until thick but do
not boil; cool and stir in salt. Makes 2 cups.

Reunion Broccoli Salad

Samantha Starks
Madison, WI

*Try adding raisins, sunflower seeds, red onion…almost anything
is good in this unbeatable salad!*

2 c. mayonnaise
1 c. sugar
2 T. vinegar
2 c. celery, chopped
2 bunches broccoli, chopped
1/2 c. green onions, chopped

2 c. slivered almonds
2 c. green grapes, halved
2 c. red grapes, halved
1 lb. bacon, crisply cooked and
  crumbled

Combine mayonnaise, sugar and vinegar together in a small bowl; set
aside. Mix remaining ingredients together. Toss with dressing; mixing
well. Refrigerate at least 4 hours before serving. Makes 20 servings.

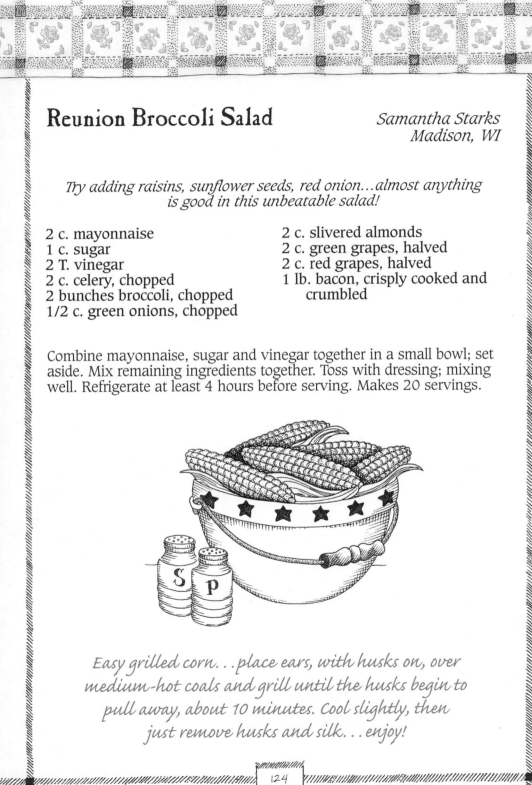

*Easy grilled corn…place ears, with husks on, over
medium-hot coals and grill until the husks begin to
pull away, about 10 minutes. Cool slightly, then
just remove husks and silk…enjoy!*

Cheesy Carrot Casserole

Linda Seidel
Reading, PA

Mom was right...vegetables are good, and good for you!

2 onions, finely chopped
2 T. margarine
1/4 t. dry mustard
1/8 t. pepper
1/2 t. celery salt
1/4 c. all-purpose flour

2 c. milk
12 carrots, peeled, sliced and
  cooked
8-oz. pkg. shredded Cheddar
  cheese
1/4 c. bread crumbs

Sauté onions in margarine; stir in mustard, pepper and celery salt. Add flour and milk, stirring until combined. Cook over medium heat until thickened; set aside. Layer half the carrots in a greased 1-1/2 quart baking dish; top with half the cheese then half the white sauce; repeat layers. Top with bread crumbs and bake at 350 degrees for 20 minutes or until golden and bubbly on top. Serves 6.

DELUXE
BADMINTON SET
· for the lawn ·

There's bound to be games at a family reunion like softball, volleyball, tag, hide & seek...be sure to keep your camera close at hand to capture all the family fun.

Cheddar-Spinach Bake

Grace Burns
Vienna, OH

Even our grandchildren will eat spinach in this yummy casserole!

2 10-oz. pkgs. frozen chopped
    spinach, cooked and drained
2 c. long grain rice, cooked
8-oz. pkg. Cheddar cheese
4 eggs, beaten
2/3 c. milk
1/2 c. onion, finely chopped

4 T. fresh parsley, chopped
4 T. butter, softened
1 t. garlic salt
1 t. Worcestershire sauce
1/2 t. dried thyme
1/4 t. ground nutmeg

Combine ingredients together; pour into a 2-quart lightly greased baking dish. Cover and bake at 350 degrees for 20 minutes; uncover, bake 20 to 25 minutes longer. Makes 8 to 10 servings.

To make sure there's plenty of room for all the homemade goodies, don't take up picnic table space with plates, cups, napkins and silverware. Stack them in a child's wagon and they can go anywhere they're needed!

Garden Fresh Pasta Salad

John Alexander
New Britain, CT

You can't go wrong with pasta salad...if you don't like green pepper or cucumber, toss in another favorite vegetable. It's almost fool-proof.

12-oz. pkg. rainbow pasta
1 cucumber, chopped
3 tomatoes, chopped
1 onion, chopped
1 green pepper, chopped
3/4 c. oil
1 t. dried parsley flakes

1-1/2 c. sugar
1-1/2 c. vinegar
2 t. mustard
1 t. salt
1 t. pepper
1 t. seasoned salt
1 t. garlic salt

Cook pasta according to package directions; set aside. In a large bowl, combine all remaining ingredients; gently fold in pasta. Refrigerate until chilled. Makes 6 to 8 servings.

Perfect for a family reunion. . . use spray adhesive to attach color copies of favorite photos to a kite form, then tie on brightly colored ribbons for a tail. Place in the center of the table for guests to admire. How fun!

Mini Apple Muffins

Kristina Carr
Pompano Beach, FL

Bite-size muffins that are just right for snacking.

2 c. all-purpose flour
1-1/2 t. cinnamon
1/2 t. salt
1 T. baking powder
6 T. butter
1/2 c. brown sugar, packed

2 eggs
15-oz. box raisins
1/2 c. chopped walnuts, optional
1 apple, peeled, cored and diced

Combine flour, cinnamon, salt and baking powder in a medium mixing bowl; set aside. Melt butter in a saucepan and add brown sugar; remove from heat when the sugar is dissolved. Add eggs and brown sugar mixture to flour mixture, blending well. Stir in raisins; blend until dough is smooth. Add walnuts, if desired, and apple; stir into muffin mix. Grease mini muffin pans and fill each 2/3 full. Bake each muffin pan separately at 400 degrees for 15 minutes or until golden brown. Makes 24.

Clever idea. . .use a garden cloche to keep pesky insects away from a plate of cookies or loaf of bread!

Blueberry Biscuits

Joyce Varney
Windham, ME

If you can get them, wild blueberries taste great in this recipe.

4 c. all-purpose flour
1 t. baking soda
2 t. cream of tartar
1 t. salt

4 T. shortening
1 c. molasses
2 c. blueberries
1 c. milk

Combine flour, baking soda, cream of tartar, salt and shortening together. Add molasses; carefully fold in blueberries with enough milk to moisten. Drop by tablespoonfuls onto an ungreased baking sheet; bake at 425 degrees for 10 minutes. Makes 2 dozen.

Pan Free

Anna Tondino
Simi Valley, CA

Just brush pans generously and baked goods come right out!

3 T. all-purpose flour
3 T. cornstarch

1/2 c. shortening

Mix ingredients together; use to grease your cake and muffin baking pans. After baking, allow to cool 10 minutes or more; invert and baked goods will release with ease.

No time to roll and cut biscuits? Just drop the dough from a tablespoon onto lightly oiled baking sheets.

Seafood Delight

Carol McMullin
Vista, CA

*When we were both working, this dinner was prepared
by my husband on his day to cook. I've since retired,
but it still remains a favorite!*

1/2 green pepper, thinly sliced
1/2 onion, sliced
8 mushrooms, sliced
2 T. olive oil
1/2 lb. scallops
1/2 lb. shrimp, peeled and
    deveined

1 clove garlic, chopped
4 T. butter
1-1/2 lbs. pasta, cooked
salt and pepper to taste

Combine peppers, onions, mushrooms and olive oil in a saucepan;
cover tightly with aluminum foil and simmer for 10 minutes. Remove
covering and add scallops; cook, covered, for 5 minutes. Add shrimp
and cook, covered, for another 5 minutes. In a separate pan, sauté
garlic in butter; set aside. Place cooked pasta in a large bowl; pour
seafood mixture and garlic butter over pasta and toss well. Salt and
pepper to taste. Makes 4 to 6 servings.

*We all want to exchange recipes at family get-togethers, so
drop a note in the mail ahead of time asking everyone to jot
theirs down and make lots of extra copies to share.*

Strawberry-Spinach Salad

Tonya Sheppard
Galveston, TX

Try this with homemade raspberry vinegar for a really fresh taste.

1 bunch spinach leaves, torn
1-1/2 c. strawberries, hulled
   sliced and divided
1 to 2 green onions, chopped
1/3 c. almonds, toasted

1/2 c. non-fat vanilla yogurt
2 T. raspberry vinegar
2 T. poppy seed
2 t. sugar

Place spinach leaves, one cup strawberries, green onions and toasted almonds in large salad bowl; set aside. Purée yogurt, vinegar, poppy seed, remaining strawberries and sugar in blender; toss with salad mixture before serving. Serves 6.

Raspberry Vinegar

Gail Prather
Bethel, MN

One of my favorite ways of preserving summer berries is by making flavored vinegars. This recipe's a sure winner!

2 c. raspberries, fresh or frozen
2 T. sugar

2 c. white wine vinegar

Heat raspberries and sugar in a saucepan over low heat until sugar dissolves, stirring often; cool. Blend raspberry mixture and vinegar together; strain through a fine sieve, discarding solids. Store in an airtight container and refrigerate until ready to use. Makes about one pint.

Banana-Sour Cream Loaf

Gwen Mason
Garrettsville, OH

Great sliced and topped with cream cheese or toasted with butter.

2/3 c. butter
1-1/3 c. sugar
2 eggs
1-1/2 c. bananas, mashed
2-1/4 c. all-purpose flour

1 t. baking powder
1 t. baking soda
1/2 t. salt
1/2 c. sour cream
1 c. chopped nuts

Cream butter and sugar together; add eggs and bananas, beat until smooth. In a separate bowl, sift flour, baking powder, baking soda and salt together. Add dry mixture alternately with sour cream to banana mix, blend well. Fold in nuts and pour into a greased 9"x5" loaf pan; bake at 350 degrees for 45 minutes. Makes 8 servings.

Tuck family photos into florist card holders and arrange along with fresh flowers to use as a table centerpiece. . . what a wonderful way to celebrate your family.

Praline Pound Cake

Beth Livengood
Landis, NC

Unbelievably good served with a side of vanilla ice cream.

1 lb. butter, softened	4 c. all-purpose flour
2 c. sugar	3/4 c. pecans, finely chopped
1 c. brown sugar, packed	3/4 c. milk
6 eggs	1 T. vanilla extract

Cream butter with sugars; add eggs, one at a time, beating well after each addition. In a separate bowl, toss flour with pecans. Alternate adding flour and milk to butter mixture, beginning and ending with flour. Stir in vanilla; beat batter for 5 minutes. Pour into a greased and floured 10" tube baking pan; bake at 300 degrees for 1-1/2 hours. Cool in baking pan for 15 minutes then remove to a rack to cool; poke holes in the top with a fork. Prepare glaze and drizzle over pound cake. Makes 12 servings.

Glaze:

1 c. brown sugar, packed	1/2 c. butter
1 c. chopped pecans	

Combine ingredients in a saucepan; bring to a boil over medium heat.

Oh, cakes and friends we should choose with care. Not always the fanciest cake that's there, is the best to eat! And the plainest friend is sometimes the finest one in the end.
-Margaret Sangster

Creamy Macaroni Salad

Penny Sherman
Cumming, GA

No picnic is complete without macaroni salad!

1/2 c. mayonnaise	1 c. celery, chopped
2 T. mustard	1/4 c. green pepper, chopped
1/2 c. sour cream	1/4 c. red pepper, chopped
1/4 c. half-and-half	1/3 c. sweet onion, chopped
1/2 t. salt	8-oz. pkg. elbow macaroni,
1 t. pepper	cooked and drained

Combine mayonnaise, mustard, sour cream, half-and-half, salt and pepper until smooth; fold in remaining ingredients. Chill for at least 2 hours before serving. Makes 8 to 10 servings.

Here's a neat tip to keep salads cold. . . add water to a small plastic bowl that has a tight fitting lid; seal and freeze. Place it in the bottom of a serving bowl and spoon the salad over top.

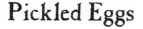

Pickled Eggs

Jen Morin
Spring Grove, PA

*This recipe's been in our family for years...it's a real
Pennsylvania Dutch treat.*

2 doz. eggs, hard-boiled, cooled
  and peeled
2 14-1/2 oz. cans sliced red
  beets, drained, reserving
  liquid

1-3/4 c. sugar
1 c. apple cider vinegar
water

Place eggs and beets in a large jar with a lid; set aside. Add water to
reserved beet juice to equal 2 cups total; combine with sugar and
vinegar. Bring to a boil in a saucepan. Simmer until sugar is dissolved;
pour over eggs and beets, being careful not to splash as the juice will
stain! Refrigerate for 3 or 4 days before serving. Makes 2 dozen.

*Hang a
clothespin bag
from the edge
of a picnic
table...just
right for
holding plastic
silverware or napkins.*

Angel Whisper Cookies

Jean DePerna
Ontario, NY

Lemony sandwich cookies...heavenly!

1 c. butter
1/2 c. powdered sugar
2 c. all-purpose flour

1 t. lemon zest
1/2 t. salt

Cream together butter and powdered sugar until light and fluffy; blend in flour, lemon zest and salt. Cover and chill for one hour. Flatten teaspoonfuls of rolled dough onto lightly greased baking sheets; bake at 400 degrees for 5 to 8 minutes. Remove to wire racks to cool. Spread filling over 1/2 of the cookies on their flattened sides; top with another cookie to make a sandwich. Makes about 2 dozen.

Filling:

1 egg, beaten
2/3 c. sugar
1-1/2 t. lemon zest

3 T. lemon juice
1-1/2 T. butter, softened

Combine above ingredients in a double boiler; stir and heat until thickened. Cool before spreading.

Animal Crackers

Lisa Watkins
Gooseberry Patch

You could drizzle these with powdered sugar icing if you like,
but they're an old-fashioned treat just as they are.

2 c. sugar
2 c. long-cooking oats,
   uncooked
1 t. baking soda
1/8 t. salt

1/2 c. shortening
1/2 c. hot water
1/2 T. vanilla extract
1/2 T. almond extract
2 to 2-1/2 c. all-purpose flour

Combine sugar, oats, baking soda and salt in a large mixing bowl; cut in shortening until crumbly. Add water and extracts; stir until blended. Add enough flour to form a stiff dough. On a lightly floured surface, roll dough to 1/8-inch thickness and cut into desired shapes. Bake on a greased baking sheet at 350 degrees for 8 to 10 minutes. Cool on wire racks. Makes about 4 dozen.

Animal crackers and cocoa to drink,
that is the finest of suppers I think.
When I'm grown up and can have what I please,
I think I shall always insist upon these.
-Christopher Morley

Dill-Cucumber Salad

Debbe Titus
Jamesville, NY

Take advantage of a bumper crop of cucumbers!

1 c. mayonnaise
1/4 c. sugar
4 t. vinegar

1/2 t. dill weed
4 cucumbers, thickly sliced
3 green onions, chopped

Whisk together mayonnaise, sugar, vinegar and dill weed in a medium bowl. Add cucumbers and green onions; mix well. Cover and refrigerate at least 3 hours or overnight. Stir well before serving. Makes about 6 servings.

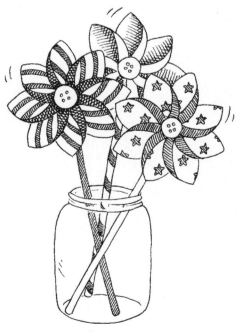

Mothers know that a child's growth is not measured by height or years or grade... it is marked by the progression of Mama to Mommy to Mother.
-Unknown

Calico Beans

Betty Lou Wright
Goodlettsville, TN

*I quickly asked for this recipe the first time I tasted it.
It's now one of those "must haves" throughout the year.*

1/2 lb. ground beef, browned
4 slices bacon, crisply cooked
   and crumbled
1/2 c. onion, chopped
1/4 c. chili sauce
1/4 c. catsup
1/2 c. brown sugar, packed

1 t. dry mustard
1 t. vinegar
16-oz. can baked beans
15-1/2 oz. can kidney beans,
   drained
16-oz. can lima beans, drained

Combine all ingredients; pour into a greased 13"x9" baking dish. Bake at 350 degrees for 40 minutes.

*Make your own game board for bottle cap checkers. Cut out
an 8-inch square of canvas and a one-inch square sponge.
Dip the sponge in paint and start laying out the game
board. It should have 8 squares, 4 stamped and
4 blank, in each row and column. The checkers
are just 2 different colors of bottle caps!*

Mom's Cherry Cream Pie

Sharon Jackson
Rye, CO

Rich and creamy...a nice change from traditional cherry pie.

1/2 pt. whipping cream
1/2 c. powdered sugar
3-oz. pkg. cream cheese

9-inch pie crust, baked
21-oz. can cherry pie filling

Blend whipping cream, powdered sugar and cream cheese together until smooth. Pour into cooled pie crust and top with cherry pie filling; chill until set. Makes 8 servings.

Whenever flower bulbs are divided or cuttings taken, share them with family. It's so special to have a garden filled with Grandma's irises or Mom's herbs...a touching way to be reminded of your family roots.

Crybaby Cookies

Linda Choudoir
Columbus, WI

If my kids were being fussy I'd ask them if they wanted some crybaby cookies...it always got a smile.

2-1/2 c. all-purpose flour
2 t. baking soda
1/2 t. ground cloves
1-1/2 t. allspice
1-1/2 t. cinnamon

1-1/4 t. ground ginger
3/4 c. butter
1-1/2 c. sugar, divided
1 egg
4 T. molasses

Sift together flour, baking soda, cloves, allspice, cinnamon and ginger; set aside. Cream butter with one cup sugar; add egg and mix well. Blend flour mixture into sugar mix; add molasses and mix well. Chill dough. Roll into 1/2-inch balls; dip in remaining sugar and place on a lightly greased baking sheet. Bake at 375 degrees for 10 minutes. Makes 2 dozen.

Once in a young lifetime one should be allowed to have as much sweetness as one can possibly want and hold.
-Judith Olney

Grandpa's Favorite Chili

Laura Witt
Goldsboro, NC

Grandpa Loveless passed this recipe down to Mom and now I make it too. Don't tell anyone what the secret ingredient is until they've tasted it…they'll love it!

1-1/2 lbs. ground beef, browned
2 15-oz. cans pinto beans
1 onion, chopped
1 green pepper, chopped

6-oz. can tomato paste
14-1/2 oz. can stewed tomatoes
4 T. chili powder
3 T. baking cocoa

Combine ingredients together in a large stockpot; simmer until beans and vegetables are tender, about one hour. Serves 6.

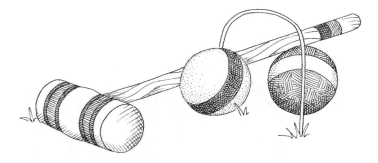

Convert a canvas tool bag into a carry-all for picnic supplies. Use the side pockets to carry napkins, silverware, glasses and condiments, then tuck plates and the tablecloth inside.

Flaky Onion Biscuits

Kristine Marumoto
Sandy, UT

Just for fun, let the kids cut these out with their favorite cookie cutters.

2 c. all-purpose flour
1 T. baking powder
1 T. sugar
3/4 t. salt
3-oz. pkg. cream cheese

1/4 c. shortening
1/2 c. green onion, finely
   chopped
2/3 c. milk

Combine flour, baking powder, sugar and salt in a medium bowl; cut in cream cheese and shortening until mixture resembles coarse crumbs. Stir in green onions. Make a well in center of flour mixture; add milk, stirring only until dough begins to stick and forms a ball. Turn dough onto well-floured surface. Knead dough gently 10 to 15 times. Roll or pat dough to 1/2-inch thickness. Cut out dough with 3-inch biscuit cutter. Place biscuits 2 inches apart on an ungreased baking sheet. Bake at 450 degrees for 10 to 12 minutes or until golden brown. Makes 8 servings.

Give extra taste to recipes that use cream cheese by trying one that's flavored...chive, garlic, jalapeño or sun-dried tomato...yummy!

Tangy Deviled Eggs

Jo Ann

You just can't have a family reunion without deviled eggs!

4 eggs, hard-boiled, cooked and peeled	1 t. onion, minced
	1/3 c. mayonnaise
1 t. prepared horseradish	1/4 t. celery salt

Slice eggs in half lengthwise and remove yolks. Mince yolks in a small mixing bowl; combine with horseradish, onion, mayonnaise and salt. Spoon mixture into egg white halves; keep chilled. Makes 8 servings.

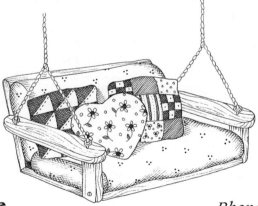

Salt Substitute

Rhonda Settle
Lubbock, TX

Try this for a little dash of flavor.

1 t. dried basil	1 T. dry mustard
5 t. onion powder	1 t. dried thyme
1 T. garlic powder	1/2 t. white pepper
1 T. paprika	1/2 t. celery seed

Combine all ingredients in an empty salt shaker and store in a cool, dry place. Makes about 1/4 cup.

Steak & Onion Pie

Tracey Clevenger
Clymer, PA

Try substituting tiny pearl onions, just as tasty
and will save prep time.

1 c. onion, diced
1/2 c. shortening
1 lb. round steak, cubed
1/8 t. ground ginger
2 t. salt
1-1/2 c. boiling water

1/2 c. all-purpose flour
1/2 t. paprika
1/8 t. allspice
1/8 t. pepper
2 c. potatoes, diced

Sauté onion in shortening until tender; set onion aside and reserve shortening. Toss meat with ginger, salt, flour, paprika, allspice and pepper; brown in reserved shortening. Add boiling water; cover and simmer 45 minutes. Add potatoes; simmer 10 minutes. Pour into an 8"x8" greased baking dish; place cooked onion on top. Cover with egg crust; bake at 450 degrees for 30 minutes. Serves 6.

Egg Crust:

1 c. all-purpose flour
1/3 c. shortening

1/2 t. salt
1 egg, beaten

Combine flour, salt and shortening; add egg. Mix thoroughly. Roll out slightly larger than top of casserole dish.

Life, love and laughter…what priceless
gifts to give our children.
-Phyllis Dryden

Garden Relish

*Mary Ann Nemeck
Springfield, IL*

*I found this recipe in a magazine almost 35 years ago and haven't
seen one like it since. Serve it in a clear glass bowl
so all the colors show through.*

1/2 head cauliflower, sliced
2 carrots, sliced
2 stalks celery, sliced
1 green pepper, sliced
4-oz. jar stuffed green olives,
   drained
3/4 c. wine vinegar

1/2 c. olive oil
2 T. sugar
1 t. salt
1/2 t. dried oregano
1/4 t. pepper
1/4 c. water

Combine ingredients together in a large saucepan; bring to a boil,
stirring occasionally. Reduce heat and simmer covered for 5 minutes;
let cool. Refrigerate at least 24 hours. Drain before serving. Makes
about 3 cups.

*A new twist on s'mores... melt peanut butter cups between
chocolate graham crackers!*

Quick & Easy Garden Pickles

Jayne Ash
Park Hill, OK

Pickles will keep refrigerated for 6 weeks...if they last that long!

8 c. cucumbers, sliced
2 c. onions, sliced
1 c. red bell pepper, sliced
1 T. salt

2 c. granulated sugar
1-1/2 c. white vinegar
2 t. celery seed
2 t. mustard seed

In a large bowl, combine cucumbers, onions, and red pepper; sprinkle with salt and toss to coat. Let stand one hour; drain. In a medium bowl, combine sugar, vinegar, celery seed and mustard seed; stir until sugar is dissolved. Place cucumber mixture in non-metallic container; pour vinegar mixture over cucumbers. Cover and chill for at least 24 hours to blend flavors. Makes 8 cups.

Tall window shutters are so nice for displaying family photos...just tuck them inside the slats!

Three-Layer Chocolate Cake

Pam Vienneau
Derby, CT

A chocolate lover's dream dessert.

1 c. butter, softened
1-3/4 c. sugar
1 T. vanilla extract
3 eggs
1 c. baking cocoa

1 t. baking soda
1/4 t. salt
2-1/4 c. all-purpose flour
1-1/2 t. baking powder
1-3/4 c. milk

Cream butter, sugar and vanilla together in a large mixing bowl until light and fluffy. Add eggs; beat well and set aside. Sift together all dry ingredients and alternately add with milk to sugar mixture. Divide evenly into 3 greased 9" round cake pans; bake at 350 degrees for 25 to 30 minutes. Cool 10 minutes in pan. When completely cool, frost with fudge frosting. Makes 12 servings.

Fudge Frosting:

1 c. butter, softened
4 c. powdered sugar
1/2 c. baking cocoa

2 t. vanilla extract
4 to 5 T. milk

Combine all of the above ingredients together in a large mixing bowl; beat with electric mixer until smooth.

Spoon ice cream toppings like jimmies, sprinkles, nuts, chocolate chips and candies into muffin tin cups...they'll be separated and easy for little ones to help themselves and top their own sundaes.

Church Socials

Barbecue Spare Ribs

Anna McMaster
Portland, OR

*Big, colorful bandannas make terrific lap-size
napkins...a must for these juicy ribs.*

4 lbs. spare ribs
1/2 c. dried minced onion
1 T. salt
1 T. pickling spice
1-1/2 c. water
1 c. catsup

3/4 c. chili sauce
1/4 c. brown sugar, packed
1-1/2 T. Worcestershire sauce
1 T. celery seed
2 t. dry mustard
1/2 t. garlic powder

Place ribs in an 8-quart Dutch oven; add onion, salt, pickling spice
and enough water to cover ribs. Cover and parboil ribs one hour. In a
separate saucepan, combine water, catsup, chili sauce, brown sugar,
Worcestershire sauce and seasonings. Bring to a boil; reduce heat
and simmer 5 minutes. Place ribs in an ungreased 13"x9" baking pan.
Pour barbecue sauce over ribs. Bake at 325 degrees for one hour or
until tender. Turn ribs in sauce at least once during baking time.
Serves 4.

*Hosting a summertime barbecue will guarantee a big
turnout of family & friends! Load grills with chicken, ribs,
brats, burgers and hot dogs, then just ask guests to bring
their favorite side or dessert to share. Add a
game of softball and it's a winner!*

Artichoke Pasta Salad

Roseann Papadatos
Copiaque, NY

Try different shapes of pasta to give this salad a new spin!

1-lb. pkg. corkscrew pasta
7-oz. jar sliced red peppers
6-oz. jar marinated artichokes
8-oz. jar black olives

15 slices pepperoni
1/2 lb. cubed Cheddar cheese
salt and pepper to taste
1 T. oil

Cook pasta according to package directions, al dente but not soft. Drain and rinse in cold water. Add the next 5 ingredients and toss, gently. Salt and pepper to taste; add oil. Let marinate 2 to 4 hours. Makes 6 to 8 servings.

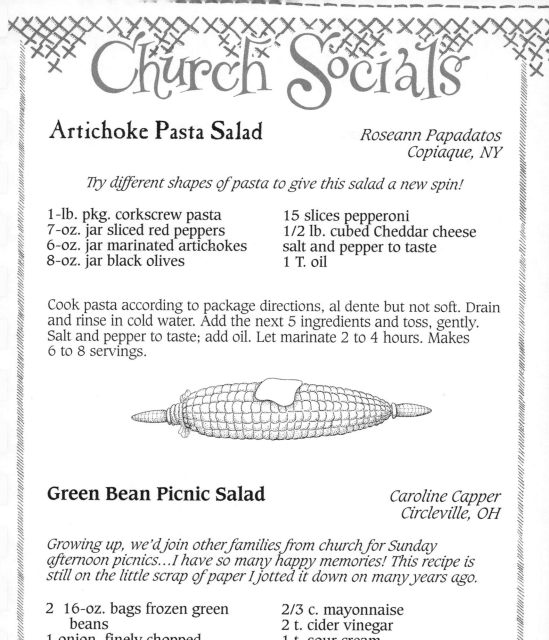

Green Bean Picnic Salad

Caroline Capper
Circleville, OH

Growing up, we'd join other families from church for Sunday afternoon picnics...I have so many happy memories! This recipe is still on the little scrap of paper I jotted it down on many years ago.

2 16-oz. bags frozen green
    beans
1 onion, finely chopped
1 T. fresh sage, chopped

2/3 c. mayonnaise
2 t. cider vinegar
1 t. sour cream
3 oz. crumbled blue cheese

Cook green beans until crisp-tender, about 8 minutes; drain and set aside. Mix remaining ingredients; toss with beans and chill. Serves 8 to 10.

Red Beans & Rice

Jennifer Clingan
Fairborn, OH

We like this served with a side of cornbread or hush puppies.

1 lb. Kielbasa sausage, sliced
1 onion, chopped
1 green pepper, chopped
1 clove garlic, minced
2 15-1/2 oz. cans kidney beans, drained

14-1/2 oz. can tomatoes, chopped
1/2 t. dried oregano
1/2 t. pepper
4 c. rice, cooked

Cook sausage over low heat 5 to 8 minutes. Add onion, green pepper and garlic; sauté until tender. Mix in beans, tomatoes and seasonings; simmer, uncovered, 20 minutes. Spoon over rice to serve. Makes 4 to 6 servings.

Setting small metal pails of citronella candles outside will discourage pesky mosquitoes...dress them up with some decorative magnets!

Louisiana Hush Puppies

Kellie Cook
Vinton, LA

Very easy and so good!

1-1/2 c. cornmeal
1/2 c. all-purpose flour
1 onion, chopped
1/2 c. green onion, chopped
1 egg
1/8 t. salt

2 T. baking powder
1/2 t. baking soda
1 c. buttermilk or milk
4 T. oil
hot pepper sauce to taste
oil for deep-frying

Combine all ingredients; stir well. Add enough oil to a deep-fryer to equal 3 inches. Deep-fry spoonfuls of batter until browned; drain and serve. Makes 24.

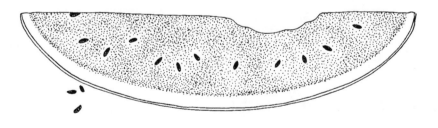

A White Elephant Swap is always fun! Ask everyone to bring something they'd like to get rid of...the sillier the better! Pull numbers from a hat and whoever has number one gets to choose his or her favorite item. Continue choosing until all the goodies are gone.

Garden-Fresh Catsup

Claire Bertram
Lexington, KY

A sweet and spicy flavor…so much better than anything from the grocery store.

3 lbs. tomatoes, peeled and
    chopped
1 onion, peeled and diced
1/2 c. vinegar
1/2 c. sugar
1 t. salt

1 t. paprika
1 t. pepper
1/2 t. nutmeg
1/4 t. ground cloves
1 T. chili sauce

Mix all ingredients together in a large stockpot; bring to a boil then let simmer for 20 minutes. Store in refrigerator up to 2 weeks. Makes 2, one-quart jars.

Brown Sugar Mustard

Dana Cunningham
Lafayette, LA

It's brown sugar taste is great on Italian sausage or brats!

1/2 c. dry mustard
1/2 c. cider vinegar
2 eggs

1/4 c. brown sugar, packed
1/8 c. oil
1/2 t. Worcestershire sauce

Blend mustard and vinegar together in a double boiler; add eggs and whisk until smooth. Stir in remaining ingredients; simmer 5 minutes. Cool and pour into a covered jar. Keep refrigerated. Makes one cup.

Church Socials

Bacon-Wrapped Burgers

Carol Burns
Gooseberry Patch

There's nothing like the aroma of burgers grilling!

1-1/2 lbs. ground beef	1/2 t. dried rosemary
1/2 t. salt	3 T. catsup
1/4 t. pepper	3 T. water
2 T. fresh basil, chopped	6 slices bacon

Combine all of the ingredients except the bacon in a mixing bowl; form the mixture into 6 patties, 3-1/2 inches in diameter and one-inch thick. Wrap a bacon slice around each and secure with a small metal skewer or toothpick. Broil or grill the patties 5 inches from heat for 5 minutes on each side for medium doneness. Remove skewers or toothpicks before serving. Makes 6 servings.

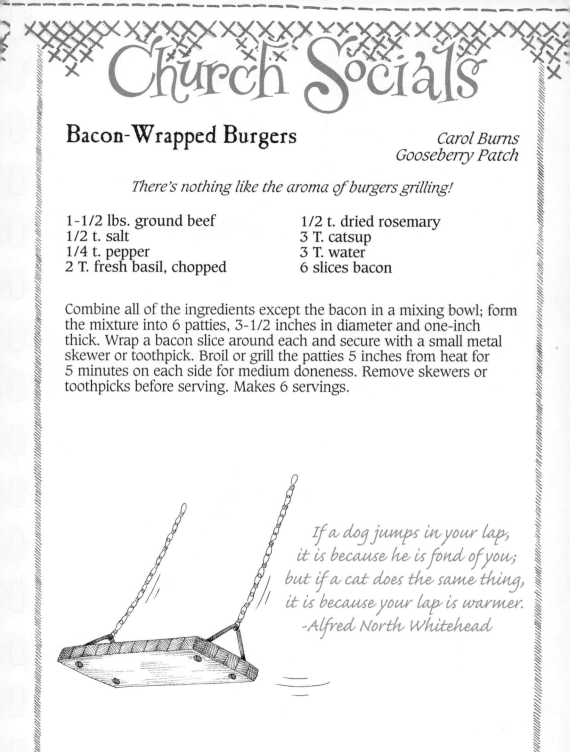

If a dog jumps in your lap,
it is because he is fond of you;
but if a cat does the same thing,
it is because your lap is warmer.
-Alfred North Whitehead

Picnic Coleslaw

Kim Faulkner
Gooseberry Patch

Creamy and slightly sweet.

4 c. cabbage, shredded
1/2 c. carrot, shredded
1/4 c. green pepper, finely
    chopped
1-1/2 T. apple cider vinegar

3 t. sugar
1-1/2 t. celery seed
1/4 t. salt
1/2 c. mayonnaise

Toss cabbage, carrot and green pepper together in a large mixing bowl. In a separate mixing bowl, combine vinegar, sugar, celery seed, salt and mayonnaise, mixing well; pour over cabbage mix. Toss lightly to evenly coat; cover and chill. Toss again before serving. Makes 8 servings.

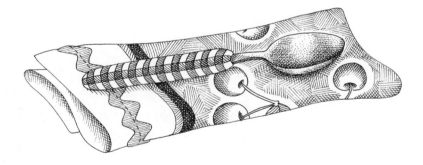

Socials are all about bringing family & friends together, so scatter disposable cameras on tables & chairs to encourage lots of picture taking!

Church Socials

Crunchy Pea Salad

Gina Yurevich
Springfield, IL

A favorite for many years...one taste and you'll see why!

10-oz. pkg. frozen peas, cooked
   and cooled
1/2 onion, chopped
1 head lettuce, finely shredded
1/2 t. sugar, divided

1 c. mayonnaise
1/4 c. grated Parmesan cheese
3-1/4 oz. jar bacon bits
1-1/2 c. seasoned croutons

Combine peas and onion; set aside. Layer half the lettuce in a
13"x9" serving dish; spread half the pea mixture on top. Sprinkle
1/4 teaspoon sugar over the peas. Repeat layers one more time.
Spread mayonnaise over the last layer and sprinkle with cheese and
bacon bits; chill. Before serving, top with croutons. Makes
12 servings.

If the ladies' group is getting together for lunch, cover tables with cotton sheets in soft sherbet colors and fill vintage teapots with pink and blue hydrangeas for centerpieces...so cozy.

Sweet Onion Casserole

Jean Barris
Bowling Green, FL

Tastes just like onion rings!

1/2 c. butter
5 sweet onions, thinly sliced into
    rings
1 c. fresh Parmesan cheese,
    grated and divided

20 round buttery crackers,
    crushed and divided

Melt butter in a large skillet; sauté onions until tender. Pour into a greased 2-quart baking dish; sprinkle with 1/2 cup cheese and half the crushed crackers. Repeat cheese and cracker layers; bake at 325 degrees for 30 minutes. Serves 8.

Add a little something special when eating outside at dusk... cover the porch with dozens of tiny white lights, hang colored tea lights from fences and trees, then after dinner, enjoy the fireflies and starlight.

Grilled Veggies

Bonnie Vaughn
North Tonawanda, NY

If you'd like, just slip vegetables on skewers, brush with marinade and cook over hot grills.

10 oz. portabella mushrooms, sliced
1 green pepper, sliced
1 red pepper, sliced
1 yellow pepper, sliced
1/2 c. olive oil
1 c. balsamic vinegar

Combine all ingredients, mixing well. Cover and marinate for 20 minutes. Fold aluminum foil into a pocket. Pour in vegetables and marinade; secure foil tightly. Grill over medium heat for 30 minutes. Makes 4 servings.

How rare and wonderful is that flash of a moment when we realize we have discovered a friend.
-William E. Rothschild

Five-Bean Bake

Deanna Krol
Nickerson, KS

Slow cookers are easily toted to socials and this recipe can be converted...just cook all ingredients on low for 3 to 4 hours.

1/2 lb. bacon, crisply cooked and crumbled, drippings reserved
1 onion, chopped
2 16-oz. cans baked beans, drained
14-1/2 oz. can green beans, drained
15-oz. can butter beans, drained

15-1/2 oz. kidney beans, drained
16-oz. can chili beans, drained
1 t. chili powder
1/4 t. hot pepper flakes
1 c. catsup
3/4 c. brown sugar, packed

In 3 tablespoons bacon drippings, sauté onion until soft. In a 2-quart casserole dish, add cooked bacon and onion. Pour in the remaining ingredients; mix well. Bake in 350 degree oven for 45 minutes or until beans are tender. Makes 10 to 12 servings.

If time is short, keep side dishes simple and quick to fix....thick slices of tomatoes layered with mozarella cheese and drizzled with olive oil, new potatoes boiled just until tender, then tossed with butter and parsley or big bowls of fresh fruit all are simple and delicious.

Sweet Italian Sausage

Kendall Hale
Lynn, MA

Add crushed red pepper for really hot sausage!

2 lbs. ground pork
1 T. dried parsley flakes
2 t. salt
2 t. paprika
1-1/2 t. fennel seed
2 t. garlic powder

1/2 t. pepper
1/8 t. dried thyme
1/4 t. allspice
1/8 t. nutmeg
1/4 t. bay leaves, ground

Combine all ingredients and blend well. Form into patties and grill until done. Makes 8 to 10 servings.

Scoop out a watermelon half, then fill with juicy fresh fruit...strawberries, cherries, raspberries, bananas, grapes and watermelon balls...always a favorite!

Lemon-Garlic Grilled Chicken

Jennie Kolaski
Hamilton, NJ

The marinade flavors blend together to create a great tangy sauce.

4 boneless, skinless chicken
   breasts
1/8 t. salt
1/8 t. pepper
2 T. oil

3/4 c. chili sauce
2 T. lemon juice
2 cloves garlic, minced
3 T. fresh basil, chopped

Season chicken with salt and pepper; set aside. Mix oil, chili sauce, lemon juice, garlic and basil together; baste chicken. Grill chicken 10 minutes. Turn and baste every 10 minutes until juices run clear, about 40 minutes. Makes 4 servings.

Woe to the cook whose sauce has no sting.
-Chaucer

Church Socials

Pico de Gallo

Betsy Walker
El Paso, TX

We love this with warm tortilla chips or spread on grilled chicken.

1/4 c. onion, finely chopped
1 tomato, finely chopped
1 jalapeno pepper, seeded and
   chopped

juice of one lime
1/8 t. salt
1/4 c. fresh cilantro, chopped

Gently mix all ingredients together in a small mixing bowl; cover and refrigerate at least one hour. Makes 1-1/2 cups.

Marinade for Poultry

Barb Vermeer
Orange City, IA

Beware: this attracts neighbors!

1/4 c. soy sauce
1/4 c. oil
1/4 c. apple juice
2 T. lemon juice

2 T. dried minced onion
1 t. vanilla extract
1/4 t. ground ginger
1/4 t. garlic powder

Mix ingredients together; pour over 3 to 4 turkey or chicken breast fillets. Cover and refrigerate overnight. Grill over medium heat about 10 minutes on each side or until juices run clear when meat is pierced. Makes 4 servings.

Tied with gingham, little terra cotta pots are charming holders for vegetable or fruit dip, salsa or condiments.

Fudge Sauce

Gail Paradise
Wharton, NJ

For special occasions my grandmother used to serve fudge sauce on ice cream...mint chocolate-chip was the best!

1-oz. sq. chocolate
1 T. butter
1/3 c. boiling water
1 c. sugar

2 T. corn syrup
1/2 t. vanilla extract
1/8 t. salt

Melt chocolate in a double boiler; slowly add butter and boiling water stirring constantly. Bring chocolate mixture to a boil; add sugar and corn syrup. Boil 5 minutes; remove from heat and cool for 15 minutes. Stir in vanilla and salt; serve immediately. Makes 1-1/2 cups.

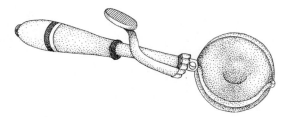

Peppermint Sauce

Stephanie Pulkownik
South Milwaukee, WI

Yummy on chocolate ice cream or blended into a milkshake.

1-1/2 c. peppermint candies,
   finely crushed

1-1/2 c. whipping cream
7-oz. jar marshmallow creme

Combine ingredients together in a heavy saucepan; cook over medium heat until smooth and creamy, stirring constantly. Remove from heat, cool and store in an airtight container in the refrigerator. Makes 2-1/2 cups.

Praline Sauce

Carol Jones
Twin Falls, ID

A sweet sauce filled with brown sugar and pecans, it's wonderful on ice cream or spooned over warm slices of pound cake.

1/4 c. butter, melted
1 c. brown sugar, packed
1/2 c. whipping cream

1/2 c. corn syrup
3/4 c. chopped pecans
1 t. vanilla extract

Combine butter, sugar and whipping cream together in a heavy saucepan. Over medium heat, stir until sugar is dissolved; add corn syrup. Continue to cook and stir until mixture thickens; add pecans. Remove from heat; stir in vanilla. Store in the refrigerator. Makes about 2 cups.

*In the sweetness of friendship let there be laughter,
and sharing of pleasures.*
-Kahlil Gibran

Vanilla Syrup

Becky Hubbard
Fredericksburg, VA

So delicious drizzled on warm baked apples or bread pudding.

2 c. water
1-1/2 c. sugar
1/2 c. brown sugar, packed
2 T. butter

3 T. vanilla extract
1/4 t. cinnamon
1/2 c. cold water
1/2 c. cornstarch

Bring water and sugars to a rolling boil in a large saucepan; add butter, vanilla and cinnamon. In a separate mixing bowl, stir cold water and cornstarch together until smooth; slowly add to boiling sugar mixture. Stir until syrup thickens slightly; remove from heat and cool. Serve warm or chilled. Makes about 4 cups.

An ice cream social is welcome relief from the summer heat. Set up an ice cream stand with big scoops of ice cream and lots of toppings... nuts, whipped cream, bananas and homemade root beer for creamy floats.

Dark Chocolate Syrup

Tami Bowman
Gooseberry Patch

Heavenly on sliced strawberries and homemade ice cream.

1-1/2 c. sugar
1 c. baking cocoa

1 c. water
2 t. vanilla extract

Stir sugar, cocoa and water together in a deep sauce pan; cover and cook over low heat about 15 minutes, stirring often. Remove from heat, cool and stir in vanilla; chill several hours before use. Makes 3 cups.

Chocolatey Popsicles

Beth Kramer
Port Saint Lucie, FL

Kids will love these frozen treats!

3-1/2 oz. pkg. instant chocolate
    pudding

1/2 c. sugar
3 c. milk

Prepare chocolate pudding following package directions; set aside. Combine sugar and milk in a medium mixing bowl; stir in pudding and blend until smooth. Pour mixture into small plastic cups or popsicle molds and freeze. When partially set, insert a popsicle stick; refreeze. Makes 8.

Best-Ever Vanilla Ice Cream

Wendy Jacobs
Idaho Falls, ID

*There's just nothing like homemade ice cream. This is just a basic
vanilla recipe, great by itself or with some fresh fruit added.*

2 qt. half-and-half
1/2 pt. whipping cream
1-1/2 c. sugar

5 t. vanilla extract
2 t. salt

Mix all ingredients together; freeze according to ice cream maker's
instructions. Makes one gallon.

*The easeful days, the dreamless nights; the homely round of
plain delights...the simple stuff of summertime.*
-Austin Dobson

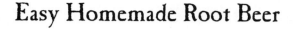

Easy Homemade Root Beer

Toni Smith
Monroe, UT

Root beer floats or root beer served in frosty mugs...either way it's great! It's so easy to make and our kids love it.

4 gal. water
2-oz. bottle root beer
    concentrate

4 lbs. sugar
4 lbs. dry ice

Combine water, concentrate and sugar in a 5-gallon plastic container; stir with a plastic spoon until sugar is dissolved. Wearing heavy gloves, carefully add dry ice. Stir until ice is completely dissolved and stops bubbling. Root beer will stay cool and fizzy if refrigerated or kept on the countertop in an insulated airtight container. Makes 4 gallons.

Combine root beer ingredients in an old-fashioned milk can and add the lid. It won't be long until the kids are lined up waiting for their turn at a very important job...sitting on top to make sure none of the carbonation escapes!

Fair-Winning Funnel Cakes

Geneva Rogers
Gillette, WY

Make this all-time fair favorite for your next gathering...a hit!

1-1/3 c. all-purpose flour
2 T. sugar
1 t. baking soda
1 t. baking powder
1/4 t. salt

1 egg
3/4 c. milk
oil for deep-frying
Garnish: powdered sugar

Sift flour, sugar, baking soda, baking powder and salt together; set aside. Mix egg and milk together; add to flour mixture. Stir until batter is smooth. Pour oil into a deep skillet to a depth of one inch; heat oil over medium heat to 375 degrees on a candy thermometer. Holding a finger over the spout of a funnel, pour 1/4 cup batter into the funnel. Release your finger and allow batter to flow into the hot oil, spiraling batter to form cake. Fry for 2 minutes on each side or until golden brown; drain and sprinkle with powdered sugar. Makes 6 funnel cakes.

Make a batch of chocolate cut-outs, then cut shapes from one-inch thick slices of hard ice cream using the same cookie cutter. Place the ice cream between two cookies, wrap in wax paper and freeze until ready to serve...homemade ice cream sandwiches!

Elephant Ears

Carol Lytle
Columbus, OH

The batter for these treats can be prepared the night before.

2 T. sour cream
1 c. buttermilk
1 egg
1 t. salt
2 T. margarine, melted

2-3/4 c. all-purpose flour
1 t. baking soda
oil for deep-frying
1/4 c. sugar
2 t. cinnamon

Spoon sour cream into a one-cup measuring cup and add only enough buttermilk to equal one cup total; pour into a large mixing bowl. Add egg, salt and margarine; blend well. Slowly mix in flour and baking soda; turn onto floured surface and knead until smooth. Let stand for 3 hours or leave in the refrigerator overnight. Divide into desired serving sizes; roll each piece out to 1/4-inch thickness. Cut slits in the center of each piece, leaving 2 halves joined at the top to make the ears. Pour oil into a deep skillet to a depth of one inch; heat oil over medium heat to 375 degrees on a candy thermometer. Fry dough in hot oil until golden brown on both sides; sprinkle with sugar and cinnamon. Makes 4 to 6 servings.

Other elephant ear toppers…toasted coconut, grated nutmeg, chopped macadamia nuts or crumbled gingersnaps…yum!

Homestyle Baked Beans

Jennifer Licon-Conner
Gooseberry Patch

So simple and easily doubled for a crowd.

16-oz. can baked beans
15-1/2 oz. can kidney beans,
   rinsed and drained
15-oz. can butter beans, rinsed
   and drained
1/4 c. tomato sauce

1/3 c. catsup
1 onion, finely chopped
1 t. dry mustard
2 cloves garlic, minced
3/4 c. brown sugar, packed
1 T. Worcestershire sauce

Combine all ingredients together; pour in a greased 13"x9" baking dish. Bake, uncovered, at 350 degrees for 30 minutes or until beans are desired consistency. Makes 12 servings.

A wildflower bouquet tucked in an unbreakable pitcher is easily toted to any gathering.

Sun Pickles

DiAnn Voegele
Mascoutah, IL

What could be easier?

6 doz. pickling cucumbers
1 onion, chopped
4 cloves garlic
1/3 c. pickling spices
1 dried red hot pepper, crushed

2 to 3 bunches fresh dill
1 qt. vinegar
1 qt. water
2/3 c. salt
2 T. sugar

Loosely pack pickles into a wide-mouth, 2-gallon jug; add onion, garlic, pickling spices and dried red hot pepper. Top with a layer of fresh dill. Bring vinegar, water, salt and sugar to a boil in a saucepan; pour over pickles. Seal with a lid; set in the sun for 2 to 3 days or up to a week. The longer pickles remain in the sun, the stronger the taste. When desired taste is achieved, bring to room temperature and refrigerate. Makes 2 gallons.

Pickling Spices

Connie Bryant
Topeka, KS

Tuck into a 2-gallon jar along with recipe for sun pickles...your neighbors will love it!

2 T. mustard seed
2 t. allspice
2 t. black peppercorns
2 t. dill seed

2 t. coriander seed
6 dried bay leaves, crumbled
2 1-1/2 inch whole dried red
    chilies, coarsely broken

Combine in a shaker jar and mix well. Makes 1/3 cup.

Children's sand pails make whimsical ice buckets for a birthday party or baby shower!

Creamy Corn Chowder

Lynda McCormick
Burkburnett, TX

This has to be one of the best soup recipes I've ever come across!

1 t. olive oil
1 t. dried thyme, crumbled
3 cloves garlic, pressed
1/4 t. pepper
20-oz. pkg. frozen corn

1 c. frozen diced hash-brown
   potatoes with onion and
   sweet peppers
14-1/2 oz. can chicken broth
14-3/4 oz. can creamed corn
1 c. milk

Heat oil in a Dutch oven. Add thyme, garlic and pepper; cook for one minute. Add corn, potatoes and broth; bring to a boil. Reduce heat and simmer, covered, for 5 minutes or until potatoes are tender. Add creamed corn and milk; heat through but do not boil. Makes 6 servings.

Show off colorful bean salads and slaws by serving them in big one-gallon canning or pickle jars. Just wrap each jar in napkins or dish towels to protect them on the journey to the social.

Turkey Pot Pie

Barbara Wise
Jamestown, OH

*There are so many ways to serve leftover turkey, but
this old-fashioned pot pie is one of the best.*

4 c. chicken broth
3 carrots, peeled and cubed
2 potatoes, peeled and cubed
1 onion, chopped
1/3 c. all-purpose flour
1/4 c. plus 1 t. cold water,
    divided
1 t. salt

1/2 t. nutmeg
pepper to taste
10-oz. pkg. frozen peas
3 c. cooked turkey, cubed
4 9-inch refrigerated pie crusts,
    unbaked
1 egg

Heat broth, carrots, potatoes and onion in a large saucepan until
boiling; turn down heat and simmer for 15 to 20 minutes or until
potatoes are tender. In a separate mixing bowl, stir flour into 1/4 cup
cold water to make a smooth paste; whisk into hot broth. Add salt,
nutmeg and pepper; simmer 15 to 20 more minutes or until thickened.
Stir in peas and turkey; heat thoroughly. Unfold 2 pie crusts and let sit
15 minutes. Place one in each of 2 pie pans and bake at 425 degrees
for 8 to 10 minutes; pour in turkey mixture and top with remaining
crusts; vent tops. Blend together egg and one teaspoon water; brush
on top pie crusts. Bake at 425 degrees for 15 to 20 minutes.
Serves 16.

*The first Sunday in August is Friendship Day...what a
perfect time for a get-together!*

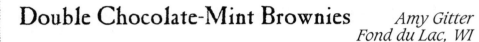

Double Chocolate-Mint Brownies

Amy Gitter
Fond du Lac, WI

Rich and chocolatey with a yummy mint center.

1 c. all-purpose flour
1 c. sugar
1 c. plus 6 T. butter, softened
   and divided
4 eggs
16-oz. can chocolate syrup

2 c. powdered sugar
1 T. water
1/2 t. mint extract
3 drops green food coloring
1 c. chocolate chips

Beat flour, sugar, 1/2 cup butter, eggs and syrup in a large mixing bowl until smooth; pour into a greased 13"x9" baking pan. Bake at 350 degrees for 25 to 30 minutes or until top springs back when lightly touched; cool completely in the pan. Combine powdered sugar and 1/2 cup butter, water, mint extract and food coloring in a mixing bowl; beat until smooth. Spread over brownie; chill. Melt chocolate chips and 6 tablespoons of butter in a double boiler; stir until smooth. Pour over chilled mint layer; cover and chill again. Cut into small squares to serve. Makes 4 to 5 dozen.

Cherish all your happy moments.
-Christopher Morley

Blondies

Leslie Stimel
Gooseberry Patch

First-rate chewy brownies!

6 T. butter, melted
1 egg
1 c. brown sugar, packed
1 T. hot water
1 t. vanilla extract

1 c. all-purpose flour
1/2 t. baking powder
1/4 T. baking soda
1/2 t. salt
1/3 c. chocolate chips

Combine butter, egg, brown sugar, hot water and vanilla; mix well and set aside. Sift together flour, baking powder, baking soda and salt in a separate mixing bowl; add to sugar mixture and blend well. Pour into a greased 8"x8" baking pan; sprinkle with chocolate chips. Bake at 350 degrees for 20 to 30 minutes; cool and cut into squares to serve. Makes one dozen.

Milk & Honey Balls

Wanda Wood
Loudon, TN

Only 3 ingredients make a quick treat.

1-1/4 c. honey
1-1/2 c. creamy peanut butter

4 c. powdered milk, divided

Mix honey and peanut butter together; gradually mix in 3 cups powdered milk. With buttered hands, roll into walnut-size balls; roll again in remaining powdered milk. Chill until firm; makes 3 to 4 dozen.

Sweet Potato Biscuits

April Jacobs
Loveland, CO

In a hurry? Just drop dough by tablespoonfuls onto the baking sheet.

29-oz. can sweet potatoes,
    drained and mashed
1/4 c. butter, softened
1/2 c. sugar
1/4 c. milk

2 t. salt
3-1/2 to 4 c. all-purpose flour
4-1/2 t. baking powder
cinnamon and nutmeg to taste

Combine sweet potatoes, butter, sugar, milk and salt; mix thoroughly. In a separate mixing bowl, sift flour, baking powder, cinnamon and nutmeg together; add to potato mixture. Mix with hands to form a soft dough. On a floured surface, roll dough to one-inch thickness; cut out biscuits and place on greased baking sheets. Bake at 350 degrees for 15 to 20 minutes or until light golden brown. Makes 3 dozen.

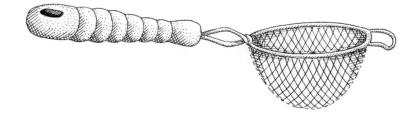

Treasure hunts can be fun for everyone! Give each person a list of items to find along with a paper or plastic bag to use as a tote. Be sure to have lots of "winner" categories so everyone gets a prize.

Old-Fashioned Apple Cider

Danelle Klaman
Fargo, ND

Refreshing served either hot or cold.

3 qts. apples, cored and thickly
   sliced
4 T. cream of tartar

3 qts. boiling water
1 c. sugar
2 cinnamon sticks

Place apple slices in a large saucepan; sprinkle with cream of tartar. Pour boiling water over apples; stir and cover for 24 hours. Strain the juice from the apples and discard apple solids. Bring juice to a boil; add sugar and cinnamon. Boil for 10 minutes longer; serve either hot or cold. Makes one gallon.

There's just nothing like a slice of warm, juicy pie. It's always a favorite and so are pie socials! Ask friends & family to bring their favorite pies to share, then be sure to have pitchers of icy milk on hand to enjoy alongside.

Shredded Chicken Sandwich

*Dairy Depot
Delaware, OH*

*A quick treat to grab on the way to the ballpark or swimming pool
when there is no time for dinner.*

50-oz. can dark and white
   boned chicken, shredded
3 10-3/4 oz. cans cream of
   chicken soup

2 c. fine bread crumbs
3 oz. dill pickle juice
1/2 sleeve buttery round
   crackers, crushed

Combine ingredients in food processor until well mixed. Heat
thoroughly and serve on buns. Makes about 40 sandwiches.

*Don't just wrap sandwiches in aluminum foil when taking
them to a social. . .make them really special. Wrap each
one in wax paper and seal with a pretty label
to identify what's inside.*

Redskin Potato Salad

Marla Caldwell
Forest, IN

Redskin potatoes give an old favorite a new taste.

2-1/2 to 3 lbs. redskin potatoes
1 c. mayonnaise
1/2 c. sour cream
2 T. Dijon mustard
8 oz. cubed Cheddar cheese

8 oz. cubed Monterey Jack
   cheese
2 c. cooked ham, diced
3/4 c. tomatoes, chopped
1/4 c. green onions, chopped

In a saucepan, cook potatoes in boiling water until tender; drain and cool. Meanwhile, combine mayonnaise, sour cream and mustard in a large serving bowl; mix well. Cut potatoes into cubes. Add to mayonnaise mixture and toss to coat. Add remaining ingredients; stir well. Cover and refrigerate at least 2 hours before serving. Serves 10.

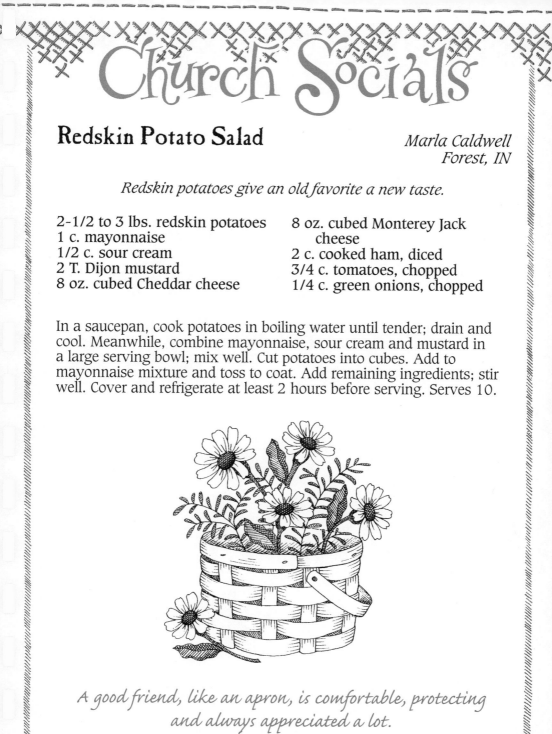

A good friend, like an apron, is comfortable, protecting
and always appreciated a lot.
-Claudia Rohling

Butterscotch Pie

Dena Dukes
Secretary, MD

A creamy butterscotch custard...try topping it with whipped cream.

2 c. milk
3 egg yolks
1/4 c. butter

1 T. all-purpose flour
1 c. brown sugar, packed
9-inch pie crust, baked

Whisk milk and egg yolks together; pour into a saucepan. Cook over low heat until warmed; remove from heat. Brown butter in a deep skillet over medium-low heat; mix in flour until smooth. Blend in sugar until dissolved; slowly add milk mixture, stirring until thickened, about 5 minutes. Pour into pie crust; refrigerate until firm. Serves 8.

On days when warmth is the most important need of the human heart, the kitchen is the place you can find it.
-E. B. White

Snowflake Cupcakes

Kathy Grashoff
Fort Wayne, IN

Wait until the kids spot these…they'll be gone in a jiffy!

1 c. butter or margarine,
   softened
1-1/2 c. sugar
3 eggs

2 c. all-purpose flour
1/2 c. milk
1 t. vanilla extract
Garnish: powdered sugar

Beat butter or margarine on medium speed until fluffy; gradually add sugar, beating well. Add eggs, one at a time, beating after each addition. Add flour to creamed mixture alternately with milk, beginning and ending with flour, mixing well after each addition; stir in vanilla. Spoon batter into paper-lined miniature muffin pans, filling 2/3 full. Bake at 375 degrees for 10 to 12 minutes or until a wooden toothpick inserted in the center comes out clean. Remove from pan and let cool completely on wire racks; sprinkle with powdered sugar. Makes about 5 dozen.

Lay a stencil over cooled cupcakes, then sprinkle on powdered sugar or cocoa, gently remove the stencil to show the beautiful pattern…a nice change from iced cupcakes.

S'more Muffins

Brenda Huey
Geneva, IN

Enjoy a campfire favorite anytime!

1 c. shortening
4 eggs
1 c. sour cream
2 c. sugar
4 T. baking cocoa
2 t. salt
3 c. all-purpose flour

2 t. baking soda
1 t. cinnamon
1 c. graham crackers, crushed
1 c. mini marshmallows
1 c. chocolate chips
Garnish: marshmallow creme,
    graham cracker crumbs

Combine shortening eggs, sour cream and sugar; set aside. Mix remaining ingredients in a separate mixing bowl; stir both mixtures together. Fill greased muffin tins 3/4 full and bake at 325 degrees for 30 to 40 minutes. Cool in pan for 20 minutes; remove muffins and spread with marshmallow creme. Sprinkle tops with graham cracker crumbs before serving. Makes 2 dozen.

Lots of communities celebrate Pioneer Day each year. Why not have your own celebration? Make tin can butter and homemade ice cream, play marbles, horseshoes and tug-of-war and make corn husk or handkerchief dolls. End the day with story telling and songs around a bonfire.

Chocolate Pillows

Elizabeth Andrus
Gooseberry Patch

A popular pastime entering into the 1950's was to gather for weekly bridge clubs. An array of delicate cookies would be offered and cookie presses became all the rage!

1 c. butter, softened
3/4 c. sugar
1 egg
2 t. vanilla extract

2-1/4 c. all-purpose flour
1/2 t. salt
6 1.55-oz. milk chocolate bars,
　　broken into squares

Cream butter and sugar in a large mixing bowl; beat in egg and vanilla. Add flour and salt, blending on low speed; chill dough. Using a cookie press with sawtooth plate, press a long strip of dough on an ungreased baking sheet. Place individual chocolate squares on dough strip leaving a small space between chocolates; cover strip with second strip of dough. Repeat with remaining dough and candies. Score dough with knife between squares of chocolate; bake at 350 degrees for 6 to 8 minutes. Cool; gently break apart at scores. Makes about 6 dozen.

Go ahead, use vintage linens to spread on buffet tables...they can always be washed and they're so much nicer than plastic tablecloths.

Polka Dot Cookies

Amy Blanchard
Ocean City, NJ

Try different combinations for these cookies...white chocolate or peanut butter chips, cashews or macadamia nuts.

1/2 c. butter or margarine
1/2 c. sugar
1/2 c. brown sugar, packed
1 egg
1 t. vanilla extract
2 c. all-purpose flour
1 t. baking powder

1/2 t. salt
1/4 t. baking soda
1/4 c. milk
6-oz. pkg. chocolate chips
1/2 c. maraschino cherries,
  chopped
1/2 c. chopped pecans

Cream butter or margarine and sugars in a large bowl; blend in egg and vanilla. Sift flour, baking powder, salt and baking soda together in a separate mixing bowl; add alternating with milk to the sugar mixture. Stir in chocolate chips, cherries and pecans; drop by tablespoonfuls onto a greased baking sheet. Bake at 350 degrees for 10 minutes. Makes 2 dozen.

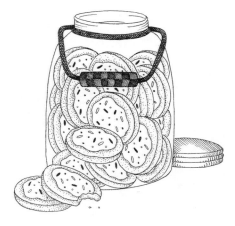

You may talk about your vases, just how beautiful they are,
but to me there's nothing nicer, than a well-filled cookie jar.
                              -Elsie Duncan Yale

Celebrations
With Family & Friends

BBQ Beef Sandwiches

Mary Hughes
Wolcott, IN

Leftovers, if there are any, freeze well.

1-1/2 lbs. ground beef, browned
1 T. mustard
1 c. catsup

1 T. vinegar
4 T. sugar
2 T. onion, diced

Combine ingredients together; simmer 15 minutes. Serve on sandwich buns. Makes 6 servings.

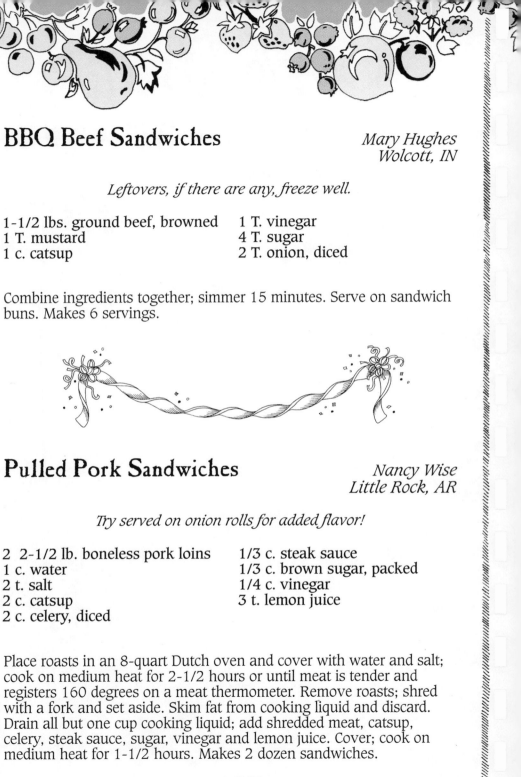

Pulled Pork Sandwiches

Nancy Wise
Little Rock, AR

Try served on onion rolls for added flavor!

2 2-1/2 lb. boneless pork loins
1 c. water
2 t. salt
2 c. catsup
2 c. celery, diced

1/3 c. steak sauce
1/3 c. brown sugar, packed
1/4 c. vinegar
3 t. lemon juice

Place roasts in an 8-quart Dutch oven and cover with water and salt; cook on medium heat for 2-1/2 hours or until meat is tender and registers 160 degrees on a meat thermometer. Remove roasts; shred with a fork and set aside. Skim fat from cooking liquid and discard. Drain all but one cup cooking liquid; add shredded meat, catsup, celery, steak sauce, sugar, vinegar and lemon juice. Cover; cook on medium heat for 1-1/2 hours. Makes 2 dozen sandwiches.

Celebrations
with Family & Friends

Sweet & Crunchy Broccoli Salad
Tina Knotts
Gooseberry Patch

For fun, serve in a red speckle pail or a child's sand bucket!

1 lb. bacon, crisply cooked and crumbled
1 bunch broccoli, chopped
1/2 head cauliflower, chopped

1 sweet onion, finely chopped
1/2 c. raisins
1/2 c. sunflower seeds

Mix all ingredients together. Toss with dressing and chill.

Dressing:

1 c. mayonnaise
1/2 c. sugar

2 T. vinegar

Mix all ingredients together and shake well.

For lasting memories, keep a scrapbook of every celebration. Fill it with photos, pressed flowers, birth bracelets…anything that's a sweet reminder. Be sure to leave room for handwritten notes, too.

Grandma's Sloppy Joes

Sue Dangler
Cecil, OH

*The savory and spicy taste will make this one of
your family's favorite recipes for any get-together.*

2 lbs. ground beef
6-oz. can sliced mushrooms,
   drained
1 c. celery, diced
2 onions, chopped
2 c. tomato juice

2 T. brown sugar, packed
1/2 c. catsup
2 T. white vinegar
1 t. chili powder
4 T. quick-cooking tapioca,
   uncooked

Brown hamburger, mushrooms, celery and onion in large saucepan or
Dutch oven; drain. Add remaining ingredients; simmer for 25 minutes.
Spoon over buns. Makes 8 servings.

Seasoned Potato Wedges

Dana Cunningham
Lafayette, LA

Easy to make and no mess to clean up!

4 russet potatoes
2-1/2 T. mayonnaise

2 t. seasoned salt

Cut potatoes in half lengthwise; cut each half into 3 wedges. Place in a
single layer on a greased baking sheet. Spread mayonnaise over cut
sides of potatoes; sprinkle with seasoned salt. Bake at 350 degrees for
50 to 60 minutes or until tender. Makes 4 servings.

Pizza Burgers

Roberta Scheeler
Gooseberry Patch

Ready in less than 30 minutes!

1 lb. ground beef
1/2 c. onion, chopped
6-oz. can pizza sauce
1 t. salt
1/2 t. dried oregano

1/2 t. dried thyme
1/4 t. garlic powder
12 hamburger buns
Optional: shredded Cheddar
    cheese

Brown beef and onions; drain. Add pizza sauce, salt, oregano, thyme and garlic powder; simmer, uncovered, for 15 to 20 minutes. Place bottom half of hamburger buns onto a baking sheet; spoon mixture on top of each bun. Sprinkle with cheese, if desired; bake at 350 degrees until cheese is melted. Makes 12 sandwiches.

A good laugh is sunshine in a house.
-William Makepeace Thackeray

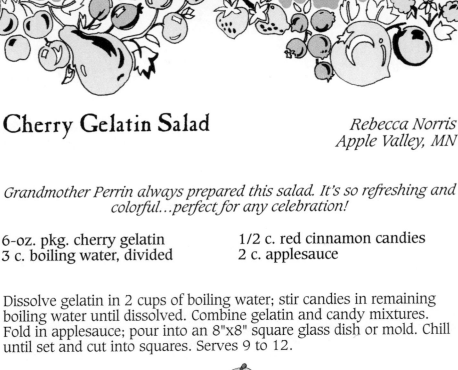

Cherry Gelatin Salad

Rebecca Norris
Apple Valley, MN

Grandmother Perrin always prepared this salad. It's so refreshing and colorful...perfect for any celebration!

6-oz. pkg. cherry gelatin
3 c. boiling water, divided

1/2 c. red cinnamon candies
2 c. applesauce

Dissolve gelatin in 2 cups of boiling water; stir candies in remaining boiling water until dissolved. Combine gelatin and candy mixtures. Fold in applesauce; pour into an 8"x8" square glass dish or mold. Chill until set and cut into squares. Serves 9 to 12.

Candied Apple Slices

Marcia Reps
Utica, MN

My kids love these...yours will too.

9 Red Delicious apples, peeled,
    cored and sliced
2 c. water

1 c. sugar
3/4 c. red cinnamon candies

Combine apples with water, sugar and candies into a large saucepan; toss lightly. Simmer for about 45 minutes or until apples are tender; stir lightly every 15 minutes. Cool then refrigerate. Makes 10 servings.

Sweet & Tart Baked Apples

*Honey Lacy
Frisco, TX*

Cinnamon and berry-filled apples taste great alone or topped with cinnamon ice cream for a real treat.

4 Red Delicious apples, cored
1 c. brown sugar, packed
1 t. cinnamon

1 c. cranberries, chopped
1 c. bananas, chopped

Place apples upright in a baking dish; set aside. Mix remaining ingredients together and spoon into the cored apples. Bake at 375 degrees for 45 minutes or until apples are tender. Makes 4 servings.

Scoop out oranges or melon halves and fill with mixed fruit or a fresh fruit salad...individual serving dishes that are very pretty for a bridal or baby shower.

Gumdrop Cookies

Karen Moran
Navasota, TX

Special to me because my mother always made these
on my first day of school.

1 c. shortening
1 c. sugar
1 c. brown sugar, packed
4 eggs, beaten
1 c. gumdrops

2 c. quick-cooking oats,
  uncooked
1 t. baking powder
1 t. baking soda
2-1/4 c. all-purpose flour

Cream shortening, sugars and eggs in a large mixing bowl; stir in gumdrops. In a separate mixing bowl, combine oats, baking powder, baking soda and flour; blend into the sugar mixture. Drop by teaspoonfuls onto a greased baking sheet. Bake at 350 degrees for 10 to 15 minutes until done. Makes 4 dozen.

Sweetheart pins make darling bridesmaid gifts. Purchase mini picture frames and glue on tiny buttons, beads or pearls. Use hot glue to secure a pin-back and wrap each in a vintage handkerchief for gift-giving. A favorite photo can easily be slipped inside... so sweet.

Peanut Butter Fudge

Brenda Doak
Gooseberry Patch

Creamy and soft...a Gooseberry Patch favorite!

1 t. cornstarch
1 T. water
1-lb. pkg. brown sugar
3 T. sugar

1/2 c. milk
1 T. butter
1 t. vanilla extract
8-oz. jar smooth peanut butter

Mix cornstarch and water; set aside. Dissolve sugars with milk and butter in a heavy saucepan. Heat until candy thermometer reaches the soft ball stage or 234 degrees. Stir in cornstarch mixture and remove from heat; it will appear lumpy. Blend in vanilla and peanut butter; pour into an 8"x8" buttered pan. Cool. Makes about 2 pounds.

Chocolate-Peanut Butter Candy

Laura Fuller
Fort Wayne, IN

Two favorite flavors combine to make a tasty candy.

1 lb. white chocolate bark,
    chopped
1/2 c. chunky peanut butter

1/2 c. semi-sweet chocolate
    chips
4 t. half-and-half

Heat chocolate bark and peanut butter in a double boiler, stirring often until melted. Coat an aluminum foil-lined baking sheet with non-stick vegetable spray and pour on melted mixture. Melt chocolate chips and cream in a double boiler, stirring until smooth. Remove from heat and pour over peanut butter layer. Refrigerate until set then break into bite-size pieces. Makes about 1-1/2 pounds.

Quick Sourdough Bread

Theone Neel
Bastian, VA

A very tasty, very old-fashioned bread can now be made quickly and easily.

3 T. instant potato flakes	1/2 c. plus 2 T. oil, divided
3/4 c. sugar	1 T. salt
2-1/2 c. warm water, divided	6 to 7 c. bread flour
1 pkg. active dry yeast	2 T. butter, melted

Mix potato flakes, sugar, one cup warm water and yeast in a large bowl. Cover and let stand overnight at room temperature. In the morning, combine 1/2 cup oil, salt, 1-1/2 cups warm water and flour; stir into the yeast mixture. Cover and let dough double in bulk; punch down and divide into thirds. Knead each third 6 to 8 times; shape into loaves. Place each loaf into a greased 8"x4" loaf pan; brush tops with remaining oil. Let rise until double in bulk; bake at 350 degrees for 25 to 30 minutes. Remove from oven and brush tops with melted butter. Makes 3 loaves.

When my mother had to get dinner for 8, she'd just make enough for 16 and only serve half!

-Gracie Allen

Grandma's Beef Stew

Kristine Marumoto
Sandy, UT

A family gathering means everyone brings their
"special" recipe…it's just expected! Here's a hearty,
traditional stew you can count on everyone enjoying.

1 lb. stew beef, cubed
2 T. all-purpose flour
2 t. oil
2 onions, thinly sliced
2 c. sliced mushrooms
2 cloves garlic, minced
2 t. tomato paste

2 c. beef both
4 c. carrots, sliced
2 potatoes, thinly sliced
1 c. canned green beans, drained
1 T. cornstarch
1 T. cold water
1/4 c. fresh parsley, chopped

Coat beef with flour, shaking off excess. In a large, non-stick pan, heat oil over medium heat; brown beef. Remove beef; set aside. Add onions and mushrooms to the pan; sauté for 2 minutes. Add garlic and sauté; drain. Stir in beef, tomato paste and beef broth; add enough water to just cover. Bring to a boil; reduce heat to low and simmer 1-1/2 hours. Add carrots, potatoes and green beans; cover and simmer 15 minutes more. In a small bowl, mix cornstarch and cold water until smooth; stir mixture into stew. Increase heat to boiling; stir until thickened. Sprinkle servings with parsley. Serves 6.

Blackberry Dumplings

*Carol Shade
Louisiana, MO*

Blackberries are only available for a short time in July, so pick as many of the plump, juicy berries as possible...you'll make this more than once!

1 qt. blackberries
1 c. plus 2 T. sugar, divided
1/4 c. water
1 c. all-purpose flour

1-1/4 t. baking powder
1 t. salt
2 T. shortening
1/2 c. milk

Combine blackberries, one cup of sugar and water in a large saucepan over medium heat; bring to a boil. In a mixing bowl, sift flour, baking powder, salt and 2 tablespoons sugar together. Cut in shortening until mixture resembles coarse crumbs; lightly mix in milk with a fork to form a soft dough. Drop dough by tablespoonfuls into boiling fruit. Simmer, uncovered, for 10 minutes; cover and simmer 10 minutes longer. Makes 6 servings.

Planning a wedding, graduation or family reunion means lots of paperwork to keep track of. Search flea markets for colorful wire dish racks...great for storing file folders and keeping all-important papers close at hand.

Great Grandma's Apple Fritters

Kristine Marumoto
Sandy, UT

Coated with a crispy batter, the inside is filled with sweet apples and juice. The only way to enjoy these is with a tall glass of milk!

oil for deep-frying
1 egg, beaten
1/2 c. milk
1 T. shortening, melted
1 c. apples, peeled, cored and
  diced

1 c. all-purpose flour
1 T. sugar
1 t. baking powder
1/4 t. salt
1 c. powdered sugar
1 t. cinnamon

Add enough oil to a deep fryer or Dutch oven to equal a depth of 3 inches. In a large mixing bowl, combine egg and milk; stir in shortening and apples. In a separate bowl, sift together flour, sugar, baking powder and salt; add to egg mixture. Mix well and drop by tablespoonfuls into 365 degree hot oil. Fry about 4 minutes or until golden brown, turning to brown all sides evenly. Remove from oil with a slotted spoon; drain on several layers of paper towels. Toss powdered sugar and cinnamon together; roll fritters in the sugar mixture. Serve warm. Makes 6 to 8.

Keep a journal filled with all the clever ideas you see in magazines for birthdays, weddings, graduations and anniversaries. Then, when it's time to plan a big event, all these great ideas will be at your fingertips!

Blueberry-Sour Cream Pancakes

Kathy Grashoff
Fort Wayne, IN

Give out of town guests a special treat...serve these berry-filled pancakes topped with whipped cream and powdered sugar.

1-1/3 c. all-purpose flour
1/2 t. baking soda
1 t. salt
1 T. brown sugar, packed
1/2 t. nutmeg

1 T. cinnamon
1 egg, beaten
1 c. sour cream
1 c. milk
1 c. blueberries

Stir flour, baking soda, salt, brown sugar, nutmeg and cinnamon together thoroughly. In a separate bowl, combine egg, sour cream and milk; add to the dry ingredients, stirring just enough to moisten. Carefully add blueberries, stirring gently to mix. Drop batter by 1/4 cupfuls onto a hot greased griddle. Cook until the surface is covered with bubbles; flip and cook until done. Makes 18 servings.

Buttery Maple Syrup

Regina Vining
Warwick, RI

Leave out the butter for a more traditional maple syrup.

2 c. water
1 c. sugar
2 c. corn syrup

1/2 t. salt
3 T. butter
1-1/2 t. maple flavoring

Combine water, sugar, corn syrup, salt and butter in a heavy saucepan; cook over medium heat until mixture reaches a full boil, stirring occasionally. Boil the syrup for 7 minutes; remove from heat and allow to cool for 15 minutes. Stir in maple flavoring; allow to cool to warm before serving. Makes one quart.

Brown Sugar Muffins

Sandra Millard
Eielson Air Force Base, AK

So simple...an ice cream scoop easily fills muffin tins with just the right amount of batter.

1/2 c. butter
1 c. brown sugar, packed
1 egg
2 c. all-purpose flour

1 t. baking soda
1/4 t. salt
1 t. vanilla extract
1 c. milk

Mix together butter and brown sugar; add egg and blend thoroughly. Add flour, baking soda and salt; mix. Combine vanilla and milk with butter mixture and mix again. Spray muffin tin with non-stick vegetable spray and fill 2/3 full with batter; bake at 375 degrees for 15 to 20 minutes. Makes 12 servings.

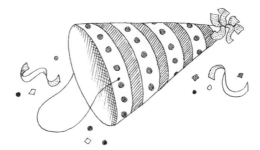

Orange Butter

Liz Plotnick-Snay
Gooseberry Patch

Spread on bagels, toast, muffins or pancakes...yummy!

1 c. butter, softened
2 t. orange zest

1/8 t. mace or nutmeg

Blend ingredients together until creamy; pack in a crock. Chill until ready to serve. Makes one cup.

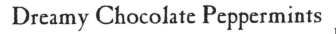

Dreamy Chocolate Peppermints

Kathy Boswell
Virginia Beach, VA

I always get requests for these...one taste and you'll know why!

1-lb. pkg. powdered sugar
2 T. butter, softened
2-1/2 t. peppermint extract
1/2 t. vanilla extract

1/4 c. evaporated milk
12-oz. pkg. semi-sweet
  chocolate chips
2 T. shortening

Combine powdered sugar, butter, peppermint and vanilla extracts. Add evaporated milk, mixing well. Roll into one-inch balls and place on wax paper-lined baking sheets; chill 30 minutes. Flatten each round to 1/4-inch thickness with the bottom of a smooth glass; chill 45 minutes. In a double boiler, melt chocolate chips and shortening, stirring often. Remove from heat. Working quickly, dip patties into chocolate; place back on wax paper and chill until chocolate hardens. Makes 3 to 4 dozen.

Caramels are only a fad. Chocolate is a permanent thing.
-Milton Snavely Hershey

Goody-Goody Gumdrops

Robin Hill
Rochester, NY

Soft and chewy...they'll bring back memories of the 5 & dime store!

3 pkgs. unflavored gelatin
1-1/4 c. water, divided
2 c. sugar, divided

1/4 t. peppermint extract
green and red food coloring

In a small bowl, sprinkle gelatin over 1/2 cup water; set aside for 5 minutes. In a saucepan, bring 1-1/2 cups sugar and remaining water to a boil over medium heat, stirring constantly. Add the gelatin; reduce heat. Simmer and stir for 5 minutes. Remove from heat and add extract; stir. Divide mixture between 2 bowls; add four drops green food coloring to one bowl and 4 drops red food coloring to the other bowl; stir. Pour into 2 greased 8"x4" loaf pans and chill 3 hours or until firm. Loosen edges with a knife; turn onto a sugared surface. Cut into 1/2-inch cubes; roll in remaining sugar. Let stand at room temperature, uncovered, for 3 to 4 hours, turning every hour so all sides dry. Makes about one pound.

When getting ready to frost a cake, set it on a lazy Susan first...so easy to turn the cake while frosting it!

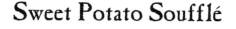

Sweet Potato Soufflé

Faye LaRosa
McKeesport, PA

No matter where I take this, it's a favorite everyone loves.

3 c. sweet potatoes, cooked and
    mashed
1 c. sugar
2 eggs
1 c. evaporated milk
1 c. margarine, softened and
    divided

1 t. vanilla extract
1 c. chopped pecans
1/2 c. all-purpose flour
1 c. brown sugar, packed

Mix sweet potatoes, sugar, eggs, milk, 1/2 cup margarine and vanilla together; pour into a buttered 2-quart casserole dish. Melt remaining margarine; set aside. In a separate bowl, mix pecans, flour and brown sugar together; stir in melted margarine. Pour mixture over sweet potatoes; bake at 350 degrees for 30 to 35 minutes. Serves 8.

"Paint" the inside of paper muffin cups with melted chocolate. Chill until firm and peel off the paper. Yummy filled with sliced strawberries!

Pork Tenderloins & Stuffing

Laura Strausberger
Roswell, GA

Homestyle best! Apples and pork are always a perfect pair.

1 T. butter	1/2 c. onion, minced
1-1/3 c. apple cider, divided	1/2 c. celery, minced
2 c. herb stuffing mix	2 1-lb. pork tenderloins
3/4 c. Golden Delicious apples, chopped	salt and pepper to taste
	4 slices bacon, halved widthwise

Bring butter and 1/3 cup of cider to a boil over medium heat. Remove from heat and stir in stuffing mix. Add the apples, onion and celery; mix well and set aside. Rinse each tenderloin and pat dry with paper towels. Slice each tenderloin lengthwise to a depth that allows you to flatten it; sprinkle with salt and pepper. Flatten one tenderloin so that the cut side is up and cover with stuffing mixture; press the other tenderloin on top, cut side down to make a sandwich. Skewer or tie the pieces together with butcher's twine, keeping the meat as flat as possible. Place in a shallow roasting pan; pour remaining cider on top. Arrange bacon slices evenly on meat. Bake at 350 degrees for 1-1/2 hours, basting occasionally with cider until meat is browned. Discard the bacon before serving. Makes 6 to 8 servings.

Tamale Pie

Sandy Rowe
Bellevue, OH

Hot pepper cheese gives this a real kick! Just substitute for Cheddar.

1 lb. ground beef
1 onion, chopped
1 green pepper, chopped
14-1/2 oz. can tomatoes
2 t. chili powder

1 t. salt
7-oz. pkg. cornbread mix
15-1/4 oz. can corn
1/3 c. milk
2 c. shredded Cheddar cheese

Brown beef with onion and green pepper; drain. Add tomatoes, chili powder and salt. Simmer for 10 minutes; pour into a 2-quart casserole dish. In bowl, stir together the cornbread mix, corn and milk, just until moist. Spoon over the meat mixture and sprinkle with cheese. Bake uncovered in a 400 degree oven for 30 minutes. Makes 4 servings.

Instead of tossing birdseed on the new bride & groom,
have guests blow bubbles...magical!

Chicken Enchiladas

Karen Hughes
Richardson, TX

I've made these for over 20 years...a delicious tradition.

1 pkg. boneless, skinless chicken breasts, cooked and diced
2 10-3/4 oz. cans cream of chicken soup
16-oz. carton sour cream
4-oz. can green chilies, diced
6 to 8 flour tortillas

1 lb. Cheddar cheese, grated
1 lb. Colby-Jack cheese, grated
1 bunch green onions, chopped
Garnish: shredded Cheddar cheese and black olives

Mix together chicken, soup, sour cream and green chilies. Spread 1/4 of mixture on bottom of 13"x9" baking dish to prevent sticking. Place 2 tablespoons mixture in each tortilla; top with cheeses and green onions. Roll tortillas closed and arrange in baking dish. Spread remaining mixture on top. Top with cheese and black olives, if desired. Bake at 350 degrees for 30 to 40 minutes. Makes 6 to 8 servings.

Clever placecards...use a marker to write guests' names on helium-filled balloons, then just tie to each chair!

Nutty Cinnamon Cookies

Sherry Doyle
Fort Wayne, IN

Crunchy, sweet and spicy.

1/2 c. butter or margarine
1 c. plus 1 T. sugar, divided
1 egg
1 t. vanilla extract
1-1/4 c. all-purpose flour

1 t. baking powder
1/4 t. salt
1/2 c. finely chopped nuts
1 T. cinnamon

Cream butter or margarine with one cup sugar. Mix in egg and vanilla; beat for 2 minutes on medium speed. Sift together flour, baking powder and salt in a separate bowl; add to creamed mixture. Chill approximately one hour. Mix nuts, cinnamon and one tablespoon of sugar in a small bowl; set aside. Mold dough into walnut-size balls and roll each in the nut mixture. Place 2-1/2 inches apart on a greased baking sheet; bake at 350 degrees for 10 to 15 minutes. Makes about 1-1/2 dozen.

I am still convinced that a good, simple, homemade cookie is preferable to all the store-bought cookies one can find.
-James Beard

Best-Ever Banana Bars

Amy Reiss
Port Washington, WI

We like to spread these bars with cream cheese icing, but they're also great just as they are, warm from the oven.

2 c. all-purpose flour
1-1/3 c. sugar
2 t. baking soda
1/2 t. salt

2 very ripe bananas, mashed
3/4 c. shortening, melted
4 eggs
2 t. vanilla extract

Combine flour, sugar, baking soda and salt in large mixing bowl; set aside. Mix bananas, shortening, eggs and vanilla in another mixing bowl; blend well. Add banana mixture to flour mixture; stir until just moistened. Pour into a greased 15"x10" baking sheet; bake at 350 degrees for 20 minutes or until center springs back when touched. Cut into bars. Makes 2 dozen.

Gather all kinds of photos, old and new, and have them transferred to a video cassette tape. What a wonderful surprise to play during an anniversary, birthday or graduation party.

Country Tomato Salad

Stephanie Washer
Lompoc, CA

Nothing compares to garden-fresh tomatoes and this summertime favorite uses the abundance from the garden.

3 tomatoes, sliced
1 cucumber, thinly sliced
1 sweet onion, thinly sliced
2 T. apple cider vinegar

2 T. water
1-1/2 t. salt
2 t. sugar

Layer vegetables in a glass bowl; set aside. Mix remaining ingredients together; pour over the vegetables. Cover and refrigerate until ready to serve. Makes 6 servings.

Be creative when displaying favorite photos. Lay a basket on its side and stand pictures in the back, or tape them to the glass of an old-fashioned swivel shaving mirror. Even the inside of a lid that has a handle. . . it acts as an easel!

Southern Fried Fish

Zoe Bennett
Columbia, SC

Served with hush puppies and slaw...a favorite here in the South.

1 c. cornmeal	2 t. cayenne pepper
1/2 c. all-purpose flour	4 6-oz. fish fillets
2 t. salt	2 T. oil

Combine dry ingredients; coat fillets on both sides with cornmeal mixture. Spread oil over baking sheet; place fish on baking sheet leaving plenty of room between each piece. Bake at 400 degrees for 20 to 25 minutes. Makes 4 servings.

Tartar Sauce

Cheryl Fitzsimon
Temple City, CA

No need to buy it in a jar...this is a snap to make!

1 c. mayonnaise	2 T. fresh parsley, minced
1/4 c. pickle relish	1/2 T. onion, grated
1 T. pimento, drained and chopped	1 T. lemon juice
	1/4 t. Worcestershire sauce

Combine all ingredients together; cover and refrigerate. Makes 1-1/2 cups.

Just for fun, recreate a nostalgic box social...serve lunch in small white cardboard boxes that have been decorated with ribbons and flowers.

Crunchy Almond-Bacon Salad

April Jacobs
Loveland, CO

*I'm always asked for this recipe, so I just make copies
ahead of time and take them with me!*

1/2 c. oil
1/3 c. sugar
2 T. vinegar
1 t. garlic salt
1/4 t. pepper
1 head lettuce, chopped

6 slices bacon, crisply cooked
  and crumbled
1/3 c. sliced almonds, toasted
1/3 c. sesame seed, toasted
4 green onions, sliced
1 c. chow mein noodles

Combine oil, sugar, vinegar, salt and pepper; mix well and chill in a covered container for at least one hour. Mix together lettuce, bacon, almonds, sesame seed and onions; toss with oil mixture right before serving. Top with chow mein noodles. Makes 12 servings.

Sweet Salad Dressing

Wendy Lee Paffenroth
Pine Island, NY

My husband, Dave, loves this...goes with any tossed salad.

2-1/2 c. mayonnaise
1/2 c. sweet relish
1/4 c. catsup

1 t. dry mustard
1 t. sugar
1/2 c. cold water

Combine all ingredients in a jar with a tight fitting lid and shake until mixed well. Refrigerate. Makes about one quart.

*A friend is someone who knows the song in your heart and
can sing it back to you when you've forgotten the words.*
-Unknown

Parmesan Brussels Sprouts

Laura Fuller
Fort Wayne, IN

A side dish full of flavor...tastes terrific with anything.

1-1/2 lb. Brussels sprouts,
    cooked and drained
3 T. butter, melted and divided
1/3 c. Italian seasoned bread
    crumbs

3 T. Parmesan cheese, grated
1/4 c. pine nuts

Place Brussels sprouts in an ungreased 1-1/2 quart baking dish; drizzle with 2 tablespoons butter. Combine bread crumbs, Parmesan cheese, pine nuts and remaining butter; sprinkle over Brussels sprouts. Cover and bake at 325 degrees for 10 minutes. Uncover and bake 10 minutes longer. Makes 4 to 6 servings.

The birthday girl and her friends will love goodie bags filled with sweet treats. Just for fun, tie bags closed with curling ribbon and a colorful jump rope they can each take home.

Three Sisters' Apple & Orange Cake *Marsha McKoy*
Rome, GA

*As a child I can remember this cake baking and the aroma that
filled the house. Named for my mother and her two sisters,
one taste takes me back to my childhood.*

1 c. shortening
2 c. sugar
4 eggs
3 c. all-purpose flour

1/2 t. baking soda
1/2 t. salt
1 c. buttermilk
1 t. vanilla extract

Combine shortening and sugar; add eggs, one at a time, mixing well
after each addition. In a separate bowl, sift flour, baking soda and salt
together. Add to sugar mixture alternating with buttermilk; beginning
and ending with flour mixture. Mix well; blend in vanilla. Divide
between two greased and floured 9" round baking pans; bake at
350 degrees for 30 to 35 minutes. Allow to cool then frost. Makes
12 servings.

Frosting:

4 apples
2 oranges

1 c. sugar
1 t. vanilla

With peel intact core and grate one apple; set aside. Peel, core and
grate other 3 apples. With peel intact, grate one orange; remove seeds.
Peel, grate and seed the other orange. In a saucepan, toss together all
of the grated apples and oranges with the remaining ingredients and
cook over medium heat until thickened, stirring constantly. Spread
warm frosting over cooled cake. Frosts 2, 9" round cake layers.

*Family photos bring smiles and make great party
invitations...so easy. Have them photocopied then just
attach to the front of plain cards with photo corners.*

Oatmeal-Raisin Spice Cookies

Kim Robertson
South Hill, VA

Easily made into a gift mix…just layer the first 4 ingredients in a wide-mouth, one-quart canning jar; packing down tightly in between each layer. Sift the next 5 ingredients and layer over oats. Attach a gift card with this recipe and baking directions.

3/4 c. brown sugar, packed
1/2 c. sugar
3/4 c. raisins
2 c. quick-cooking oats,
    uncooked
1 c. all-purpose flour
1 t. cinnamon

1/4 t. nutmeg
1 t. baking powder
1/2 t. salt
3/4 c. butter, softened
1 egg, beaten
1 t. vanilla extract

Combine dry ingredients in a large mixing bowl; add butter, egg and vanilla, mixing well. Shape into walnut-size balls; place on greased baking sheets. Bake at 350 degrees for 15 minutes or until edges are golden brown. Cool on wire racks. Makes about 3 dozen.

*An antique bird cage filled with flowers and ribbons
is a charming centerpiece for a bridal luncheon.*

Potato Lefse

Brea Watson
Medicine Bow, WY

*Short on time, serve these pastries spread with butter or sprinkled
with sugar and cinnamon...they'll be just as good.*

5 c. potatoes, cooked and
   mashed
1 t. salt

3 T. butter, melted
2 T. sugar
2-1/2 c. all-purpose flour

Beat potatoes, salt, butter and sugar together; cool until lukewarm. Stir
in flour thoroughly. Divide into 4 equal portions; cover and refrigerate
about 30 minutes. Divide each portion into 4 or 5 equal portions for
a total of 16 or 20 lefse. On a lightly floured surface, roll out each
piece into a paper-thin 10-inch circle. Heat an ungreased griddle or
non-stick pan to medium-high. Cook one lefse at a time until bubbles
are seen throughout; bottom should have the color of a flour tortilla.
Turn lefse over and bake until lightly browned. Remove from pan
to wire rack to cool; layer between sheets of wax paper. Store flat
in refrigerator in sealed container. Before serving, spread filling
generously over each lefse; fold over like an omelet and cut into
wedges or simply roll up. Avoid heating so the filling will not melt;
bring to room temperature. Makes 16 to 20 servings.

Filling:

1 lb. unsalted butter, softened
2 c. milk, warmed
2 c. whipping cream, warmed

2/3 c. honey
1 t. salt, optional

Cream butter; gradually add milk and cream, beating constantly. Beat
in honey and salt; chill 15 minutes or until slightly firm. Pour off
any liquid.

Cinnamon-Apple Squares

Catherine Ciotti
Everett, MA

Served with a dollop of whipped cream and sprinkling of nutmeg,
this makes a yummy dessert.

1-1/4 c. sugar, divided
1/2 c. plus 2 T. butter, divided
1 egg
2 c. all-purpose flour
1/8 t. salt

1 t. baking powder
4 c. apples, cored, peeled and
   sliced
1 T. cinnamon

Cream one cup sugar and and 1/2 cup butter; add egg and beat until smooth. Mix in flour, salt and baking powder; mixture will resemble coarse crumbs. Pat half the mixture into an 8"x8" baking dish; pour apples on top. Sprinkle with remaining sugar and cinnamon; dot with remaining butter. Top with remaining crumb mixture; bake at 350 degrees for 45 minutes. Makes 12 servings.

Baking a loaf of a favorite bread as a gift is so
thoughtful...why not include the recipe along with
a pretty vintage towel tied with a bow?

BBQ Meat Loaf Sandwiches

Tori Willis
Champaign, IL

*A southern favorite...old-fashioned meat loaf sandwiches
topped with coleslaw.*

1 c. barbecue sauce
1 T. cider vinegar
1 t. pepper

2-lb. meat loaf, cooked
8 onion rolls
1 c. creamy coleslaw

Combine barbecue sauce, vinegar and pepper, mix well and set aside.
Cut meat loaf into 16 slices; place 2 slices on bottom half of each roll.
Top with 2 tablespoons of sauce and 2 tablespoons of coleslaw; top
with remaining roll half. Makes 8 servings.

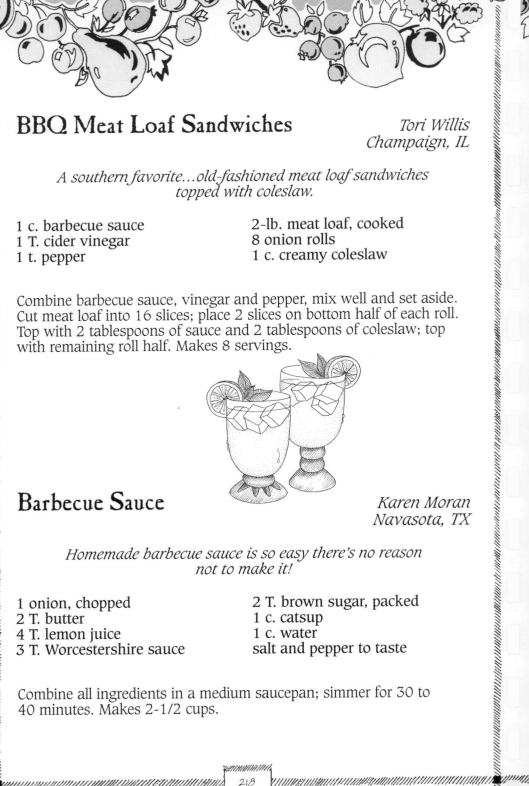

Barbecue Sauce

Karen Moran
Navasota, TX

*Homemade barbecue sauce is so easy there's no reason
not to make it!*

1 onion, chopped
2 T. butter
4 T. lemon juice
3 T. Worcestershire sauce

2 T. brown sugar, packed
1 c. catsup
1 c. water
salt and pepper to taste

Combine all ingredients in a medium saucepan; simmer for 30 to
40 minutes. Makes 2-1/2 cups.

Easy Pickled Peppers

Kristie Rigo
Friedens, PA

*A mix of hot and mild peppers that's great in salads
or on sandwiches.*

1 qt. vinegar
3 c. water
2 c. oil
2/3 c. salt
1/4 c. dried oregano
1/4 c. celery seed

4 cloves garlic, minced
8 qts. mixed hot and sweet
    banana peppers, sliced into
    rings
1 stalk celery, sliced

Combine vinegar, water, oil, salt, oregano, celery seed and garlic in a heavy saucepan; bring to a boil. Place peppers and celery in a large heat-proof bowl; pour boiling mixture over peppers and celery until just covered. Let stand at room temperature for 8 hours, stirring occasionally. Put into jars and keep refrigerated up to 6 months; makes 8 quarts.

So pretty for a baby shower...drape the gift table with receiving blankets and a whitewashed wreath trimmed with booties, socks, rattles, baby's breath and flowers.

Index

Index

Index

We've cooked up a whole collection of Gooseberry Patch® books!

Have a taste for more? Call us toll-free at
1-800-854-6673

We'll send you our latest catalog filled with snowmen, Santas, ornaments, candles, cookie cutters, gourmet goodies, calendars, giftwrap, pottery, collectibles and MORE...including our best-selling cookbooks!

Phone us:
1·800·854·6673

Fax us:
1·740·363·7225

Visit our website:
gooseberrypatch.com

Send us your favorite recipe!

*and the memory that makes it special for you!** If we select your recipe for a brand new **Gooseberry Patch** cookbook, your name will appear right along with it...and you'll receive a FREE copy of the book! Mail to:

Vickie & Jo Ann
Gooseberry Patch, Dept. Book
600 London Road
Delaware, Ohio 43015

*Please include the number of servings and all other necessary information!